Music
and
Theology

More Praise for *Music and Theology*

"Don Saliers's *Music and Theology* is...readable, informing, and construc-tive...The author combines...wisdom, good judgment, and compre-hensive knowledge of theologies old and new, and musics traditional and emerging to establish perimeters and ground rules for the needed dialogue between 'theological discourse in language and theological understanding through music.' I predict *Music and Theology* will become a standard text."
—Carlton R. Young, Professor of Church Music, Emeritus,
Candler School of Theology, Emory University,
and Editor of *The United Methodist Hymnal*

"In...poetic language, Don Saliers here addresses the wonder, mystery, and potency of music in relation to theology...This is not simply a compendium. Nor is it superficial in spite of its brevity. Serious readers will discover layers of deep meaning and will not come away unscathed. Basic questions emerge, like whether 'music offers, both in its structures and its improvisations, an image of how life may be lived.'"
—Paul Westermeyer, Professor of Church Music,
Director, MSM with St. Olaf College

"Here in this very thoughtful booklet—which is a kind of seven-movement symphony with concluding coda—Don Saliers reminds us that theology has musical dimensions and that music has strong theological overtones. Both are transformative: theology, as the encounter with God, changes and challenges us; music, as the voice of the unseen, challenges and changes us. Don Saliers challenges us to change our attitudes towards both, and in the process suggests that theology without music is 'tinkling brass' and music without theology is 'vain repetition.'"
—Robin A Leaver, Professor of Sacred Music,
Westminster Choir College of Rider University, Princeton,
and Visiting Professor, the Juilliard School, New York City

"The one who encouraged our practice of 'sung praise' continues his exquisite use of language to confirm the nature and importance of 'acoustical theology.' The blended excellence of Don Saliers's theo-logical and musical wisdom makes clear the ways each of these disci-plines wonderfully illumines the other."
—Carol Doran, professor and scholar, North Andover, Massachusetts

HORIZONS IN THEOLOGY

Music
and
Theology

DON E. SALIERS

Abingdon Press
Nashville

2007

MUSIC AND THEOLOGY

Copyright © 2007 by Abingdon Press

All rights reserved.

This book is printed on acid-free paper.

Library of Congress Cataloging-in-Publication Data

Saliers, Don E., 1937-
  Music and theology : horizons in theology / Don E. Saliers.
    p. cm. — (Horizons in theology)
  Includes bibliographical references and index.
  ISBN 978-0-687-34194-8 (binding: pbk. lay flat : alk. paper)
  1. Music—Religious aspects. 2. Theology. I. Title.
  ML3921.S16 2007
  261.5'78—dc22

                       2007002578

07 08 09 10 11 12 13 14 15 16—10 9 8 7 6 5 4 3 2 1

MANUFACTURED IN THE UNITED STATES OF AMERICA

CONTENTS

PRELUDE

Music, wrote Robert Burton in *The Anatomy of Melancholy*, "is so powerful a thing that it ravisheth the soul, the Queen of the senses, by sweet pleasure... And 'tis not only men that are affected... All singing birds are much pleased with it, especially Nightingales... and bees amongst the rest...."[1] Time would fail us to speak of the whole realm of music in the natural world, and the vast range of pleasure music brings to human beings. Anyone who loves music has experienced this "ravishing of the soul" at one time or another.

But there is so much more to be said about the power of music for the mind and heart, as well as for pleasure of the senses. Nicholas Cook, a musicologist, writes wonderingly, "If a few combinations of pitches, durations, timbres and dynamic values can unlock the most hidden contents of [the human] spiritual and emotional being, then the study of music should be the key to an understanding of [human] nature."[2] I hope to show how music may also be a key to the understanding of Christian theology. In the final analysis, music and theology may require one another. I aim to explore what is at stake in such a claim for the human intellect and heart, for body and soul.

This brief book arises from a life-long love of music and music making. Half a century as a church musician and forty years as a teacher of theology and worship have given me a broad ecumenical appreciation of the issues addressed in these pages. Music in the context of worship brings forward questions about how music is related to language about God. Yet music outside church and synagogue may also "sound" theologically relevant aspects of life. What have music and theology to do with one another? Much more than we may first assume.

As a teenager, I vividly recall playing piano for Wednesday night prayer services for evangelical congregations, and violin and clarinet in a small Sunday school orchestra in a Methodist congregation. Hymns and songs were essential to how persons in those churches conceived God. "How Great Thou Art" expressed, for many, their very experience of God in awe and wonder. For others, the classical hymn "Holy, Holy, Holy" framed their biblical picture of God. For others, "A Mighty Fortress Is Our God" expressed the heart of their faith. It was clear to me, even then, in how they sang and how they talked about God, that hymns carried much of their theology.

At the same time I was drawn to the chanting of Mass (then still in Latin) at the local Roman Catholic parish. There I found mystery in the fusion of gesture, symbol, and the sound of chant. Singing and accompanying school choirs gave me early exposure to a much larger world of choral literature. Later, during high school I formed a jazz trio, and soon began to play for dances with my father's dance band. This Saturday night and Sunday morning musical dialogue raised other issues about how music functioned in people's lives *outside* church. This led me to experiment with jazz settings of John Wesley's Morning Prayer, and to search for jazz settings of sacred texts. These I found in Duke Ellington's sacred concerts and Dave Brubeck's *Light in the Wilderness*, not to mention Leonard Bernstein's *Mass*. This yeasty mix yielded occasions to think about the connections between so-called sacred and secular music.

Learning to play sonatas by Haydn, Beethoven, and Mozart; Chopin's *Etudes*; and later Bach, Reger, Widor, and Messiaen's organ works; I encountered wordless music that took me beyond what I thought I could "hear" in religious texts. There were also the great oratorios—Handel's *Messiah*, Mendelssohn's *Elijah*; and the Passions—Bach's *St. Matthew* and *St. John*, and recently, Osvaldo Golijov's *La Pasión Según San Marcos* (*The Passion According to Saint Mark*). All of these confluences of ordered sound have formed my life in ways that cannot be said directly, but perhaps only "shown" in what the music leads to spiritually and theologically.

The invitation to write this book comes at an appropriate time in my forty years of teaching Christian theology through music and liturgy. I want to ask basic questions afresh—as if for the first time. The contemporary travail of Christian and Jewish worship in North American culture forces some of these questions. The so-called "worship wars" make serious thinking about relations between music and theology especially urgent. At the same time profound religious and theological themes set to music occur entirely outside of worshiping communities. Folk music traditions and more recent "secular" songwriters often express and explore deeply religious questions. We may find stronger prophetic texts and musical lines outside the churches than inside. While there are many voices addressing social and aesthetic issues generated at the popular level, it is all the more important to raise theological and musical questions in light of the splintered sensibility that dominates our time. The attempt to understand complex relationships between music and theology is not new, but the present situation—religious and cultural—invites a fresh inquiry into those relationships.

In these pages I seek to gain a deeper understanding of how music can be theological, and theology can be conceived as musical. How might theological discourse require music for its realization, and why do many forms of music evoke religious awareness that calls for theological interpretation?

The first chapter opens some ways of thinking about the role of sound in our experience of the world, particularly as generated by religious practices involving music. Nearly all religions employ the human voice, instruments, and acoustical images in their indigenous worship and devotional practices. The training of the ear is also a training of multi-sensory receptivity (*synaesthesia*) to the religious dimension of human life. Learning to listen is essential to a theologically formed spirituality—that is, to a disciplined way of perceiving and living in the world as a divinely created order.

The second chapter turns specifically to the Christian tradition and to what can be called "St. Augustine's ambivalence." The combination of words and ordered sound addressed to God is a form of theological communication; but it also brings a tension between words and musical form. Augustine (354–430 CE) sets the stage for a persistent debate within Christianity about words and music, a debate about theologically formed faith in the Word of God and the sensual experience of music. Theological views of music turn on where and how the boundaries between the material and spiritual worlds are drawn. Augustine's religious and reflective ambivalence is a major source of the permanent tension between spirit and the sensual that runs through the history of theology and aesthetics down to our day.

Chapter 3 takes up the question of the several tasks of theology and the multiple functions of musical value. Special attention is given to how Martin Luther's theology of music is carried forward by Johann Sebastian Bach, each yielding insight into Christian theological claims about music, and musical expressions of theology. Two twentieth-century theologians, one Protestant (Karl Barth), the other Roman Catholic (Hans Kung)—each comments on Mozart, showing how each hears Christian doctrine "sounded" musically in his music.

The next chapter explores a range of examples of poetry and doctrine in Christian hymnody. From the very beginning of Christian life and worship, hymns have been a primary carrier of theological import. Vast changes in sensibility and theological meanings can be traced by attending to the qualities and characteristics of examples from the earlier Latin and Greek office hymns to twenty-first-century hymn texts and tunes. Here we develop the sense in which a good hymn is "theology in miniature."

Chapter 5 turns to the act of singing as simultaneously theological and socio-political. Human song that arises from a paradoxical world of beauty, injustice, and human suffering is intrinsically theological. Singing has always been at the heart of social and political movements. Here I trace some connections between doxology and lament in the church's song and the role of singing in human social vision, especially movements for freedom, justice, and peace.

There is a perennial tension between so-called "sacred" and "secular" music and its theological significance. What makes this distinction less useful, and even confusing, when we study specific examples of music that carries theological and religious import? Chapter 6 addresses this question. A concluding seventh chapter reflects on musical/theological encounters with what is holy, and the human search for God. What marks those occasions when, as some may say, "heaven and earth" meet? How might certain musical experiences—with or without words—convey intimations of transcendent reality? Beauty and terror, supreme harmony and dissonance may be required for this. Why do many find that certain kinds of music reveal the deepest aspects of human beings before God—the suffering, the grace, and the glory? A brief "postlude" sounds the main theme and opens toward the reader's improvisational elaboration.

Music is first and foremost a human practice. By that I mean that it is "sounded" by voices and/or instruments by means of a disciplined set of embodied skills. Theology, too, is a practice, or more accurately, a complex set of practices. Normally theology is a verbal, conceptual practice requiring capabilities of analysis and interpretation of sacred texts and patterns of experience.

Thinking, writing, and speaking theologically about God, the world, and being human moves in both contemplative and practical modes. To contemplate God, the world, and the meaning of being human involves beholding all of life under the notion of a divinely created and redeemed order of things. It involves seeing the world as God's, or in John Calvin's phrase in describing creation, to behold the world as "the arena of God's glory." The theological act of contemplating the beauty, the goodness, and the actual complexity of what is most real may seem abstract, or at least impractical. But it need not be so. Could it be that such a beholding of the truth of things, as well as the source of goodness and beauty, may be embodied in the various arts, and most pointedly in music? Might this require attention to the dissonant, the tension-filled, and the difficult truths as well as the harmonious, the beautiful, and the praiseworthy? To these questions we will return more than once, for in music it may be possible to sound, and thus to hear, the entire range of our being before God. Could this lead us to understand how theology itself inevitably leads to musical form and realization in human song?

Chapter One

Sound, Synaesthesis, and Spirituality

Each of the human senses plays a constituent role in the formation and expression of a theologically determined spirituality. In most historic theistic traditions, seeing and hearing have a primacy of place in awakening, sustaining, and deepening awareness of the divine–human relationship. In many key disciplines of spiritual practice, tensions between what is seen and not seen, between what is heard and not heard are deliberately heightened. So, for example, in devotional practices before religious icons, sight may seem primary. Such prayer involves learning to "read" the icon as a revelatory image by which a person participates in the mystery of the divine life. For the one praying, a window into spiritual reality opens, and the person receives the "gaze" of the theological mystery given in the icon. But the immediate conditions for the gaze include touch and tactility in the devotional kiss, and the kinetic aspects of bowing and reverencing before the image. The interrelation of these senses in the full-orbed devotional practices with icons forms what we might call a *synaesthetic matrix*. The term "synaesthetic" refers to the simultaneous blending or convergence of two or more senses, hence a condition of heightened perception.

Synaesthesia is the multi-sensory receptivity of what is real. Such a matrix is found in nearly all religious traditions. This is, as we shall see, especially at the heart of ritual and liturgical participation. For Christianity this characteristically begins in sound: "faith comes by hearing."

Traditions of communal spiritual practice employ a variety of sounds to awaken, elicit, and sustain particular states of consciousness. Consider the bell in Hindu temples, Buddhism, shamanism, and Christianity. Drums and cymbals, the *shofar* and the trumpet sound and signify a range of religious sensibility in Jewish tradition, attested to in the Hebrew psalms. The sense of taste is prominent in all food rituals, from Hindu *puja* to Jewish Passover to the Christian Eucharist. Yet "tasting" can be the opening to "seeing," as in the psalm refrain, "O taste and see that the LORD is good" (Psalm 34:8). Could this be analogous to occasions in which we experience "seeing the divine" in and through sound—especially when music and text combine in ritual context? Such "tasting and seeing" require having in mind both "goodness" and having heard of this "Lord."

These initial points remind us at the outset of the ubiquity of human senses across the wide spectrum of religious and spiritual traditions. Even the most severe of interior practices presupposes the role human sense experience plays in spiritual discipline. At the same time one rarely finds one sensory mode standing alone. So in "live" musical experience we both see the musicians making the music and communicating with one another as well as hear the music. Ascetic bodily practices of restraint concerning images, whether visual or acoustical, alter the language of the senses, not only to remove distraction, but also to unveil that which transcends the ordinary content of sense experience. In fact, the discourse of spirituality characteristically speaks of another *kind* of sense—a religious or contemplative "sense" as a way of understanding reality and oneself. Cultivation of such a "spiritual sense" by which the divine glory and grace is perceived is often the aim of practices known as spiritual disciplines.

Still, one of the primary clusters of sense so crucial to much Christian spirituality is sound. In particular I am interested in how hearing sound as music, both with and without words, is central to spirituality. How is the hearing of sound itself part of the multiple senses that occur in any worship event? More especially, what is it about ordered sound as music that constitutes an *intrinsic* dimension of ritual participation? Music has been called the "language of the soul made audible." Behind this popular definition is hearing sound as an image of the deepest center of human existence. The human voice is primary in this domain of the formation and expression of a religious sense of being-in-the-world.

Saint Augustine of Hippo's ambivalence in his *Confessions* provides a good starting point. He addresses a lover's question to God:

> When I love you, what do I love? Not the body's beauty, nor time's rhythm, nor light's brightness...nor song's sweet melodies, nor the fragrance of flowers, lotions and spices, nor manna and honey, nor the feel of flesh embracing flesh—none of these are what I love when I love my God. And yet, it's something like light, sound, smell, food, and touch that I love when I love my God—the light, voice, fragrance, embrace of my inner self, where a light shines for my soul. That's what I love when I love my God! (Book X: 6,8)

How deeply intertwined the sensible joy and delight in creaturely things are in Augustine's reflections on what loving God is. He was certainly possessed of a sensibility for the beautiful, rooted here in a Platonic view of reason as *eros*, but also steeped in the concrete language of doxology nurtured in the sensory rhetoric of the psalms and Christian scriptures. What we hear, say, see, smell, taste, and touch in worship and devotion become the best analogy he can find for the soul's communion with God. This is the force of his "And yet." To say what loving God is "like" is to appeal to a whole series of senses. These seem to form a matrix of sorts. The seeming denial of the physical and sensual aspects of religious devotion is immediately forged into the description of interrelated patterns of perception. Loving God requires the interanimation of all the available senses.

3

Even more to the point here are Augustine's references to the beautiful melodies of psalm settings he heard in Milan. He wept with joy at the liberated "delights of the ear" in praying these psalms. Yet he also wishes at times to banish the melodies because of their sensual sound properties in order to attend to the words alone as the hearing of God's word (Book X: 33). As we will discuss in chapter 2, Christian tradition inherited his ambivalence toward the aesthetic dimensions of religious practices, both liturgical and devotional. Yet I contend that his tears of recognition were part of his "hearing." This ambivalence about music (the ordered sound that articulates and animates the texts of prayer) is not peculiar to Augustine. This is a central aspect of how Christian spirituality is formed. Could it be that, in order to show how sound and music shape the Christian life and sense of the divine, we must attend to the *permanent tensions* between aesthetic sensibility and holiness as transformative receptivity to God?

Perhaps we can formulate the foregoing reflections in thesis form: *Music confers upon human language addressed to God the appropriate silence and mystery required by prayer. Music is the language of the soul made audible especially as music is the performative mode of the prayer and ritual engagement of a community.* This implies that ordered sound, particularly when it animates certain texts, shapes human beings in distinctive forms of affection and receptivity. To this aspect of our inquiry we now turn.

For several years in the late sixties and early seventies my family lived in the inner city of New Haven. Our four daughters, then quite young, were taught a set of ritual songs by neighborhood friends. The children would form a circle with jump ropes. Calling out to one another across the swinging ropes, they were singing. One at a time the children would dance into the circle, hop a few steps, then dance away, all the while singing amid the whirling ropes:

"Miss Mary Mack, Mack, Mack...all dressed in black, black, black...with silver buttons, buttons, buttons...all down her back, back, back." This was a narrative ritual game. It was clear that children had to learn to accent the words just so. The movements were unmistakably improvisational—with maturation, they could become quite complex. Yet the rules were clear: "Don't miss the skips, know the words, and get the right spirit; keep the rhythm coming."

The children learned the words, the singing, and the dance together. Performing led to an ever-deepening dexterity and delight, and to communal solidarity. This image of the singing, dancing children remains for me a wonderful metaphor for the formative and expressive power of authentic liturgical participation. It is an image of vitality and of doxology. This natural language of praise is found in the fusion of ordered sound, ruled kinetic participation, and a communal sense of shared narrative.

The children were formed in a way of being together and of receiving a world of joy, precisely in the multi-sensory doing of the ritual. The sounds of the whirling rope, the sounds of feet on the earth, the squeals of delight combined with the music in performance. These formed them in a kind of understanding they have not forgotten.

The body remembers shared music making long after the mind may be dimmed. Those children participated in this *synaesthetic matrix*. Sound, pitch, rhythm, and bodily movement are found in what we human beings do in our work, our festivals, our solemn occasions of grieving, or rejoicing. Whether around campfires, in fields of harvest, or in temples and churches, the communal act of singing has formed and expressed deep human emotions. Such emotions are not simply passing states of feeling or mood; they are capacities to consent to a sense of being in the world. If music is the language of the soul made audible, then human voices conjoined in community are primary instruments of the collective soul—a medium for what transcends the immediately commonsense world. In such cases the hearing and the sound itself encode more than what is heard. This is a profoundly crosscultural fact.

Music has the power to encode and convey memory with powerful associations. Anyone who participated in or lived through the American Civil Rights movement will always hear the courage, the suffering, the pain, and the promise in "We Shall

Overcome." A whole generation of Americans who lived through World War II cannot forget the sound of Kate Smith singing "God Bless America." The African American spiritual "Sometimes I Feel like a Motherless Child" and the Appalachian song "I'm Just a Poor Wayfarin' Stranger" touch something beyond our surface longings and wishes. Words set to music are given greater emotive range and associational power than when we only speak them—much less when we only think about them. We are asked to say some things that we don't truly think we believe until we sing them, or hear them in appropriately complex activities.

Some years ago I studied the singing practices in several Protestant churches. In Bethel United Methodist Church in Charleston, S.C., I interviewed a group of older women. After asking them to identify their favorite hymns (to which they gave a standard list of hymns of the late nineteenth and early twentieth century—many of them gospel songs), I asked them why these hymns and songs were so significant. They spoke of "hearing their grandmother's voice," of "leaning against their mother's breast," or hearing the "squeak of the parlor organ," of weddings, funerals, and Sunday evening gatherings. The sounding of those hymns evoked a marvelous range of life experiences and relationships. Especially prominent was the sound of human voices, as though human existence itself was held in paraphrase before the divine, yet with all the ordinariness of non-perfection.

Anyone working with Alzheimer's patients knows that often the last way of bringing a person a present is to sing for them (and with them) songs from their childhood. This itself is a kind of metaphor for the deeper power of music to encode life, and to make it present—even in the face of cognitive diminishment.

The witness of those churchwomen also recalls Susanne Langer's notion of music as a "non-discursive symbolism." By this she means that music is not like verbal language with its specific descriptive powers of referring. Unlike "discursive" symbols, music presents us with a "language of sound" that presents and symbolizes the patterns of how we live and experience our world. Music itself offers us in the hearing—and I would add, in the singing—a pattern of how we actually experience the world and our lives. It presents to us the tensions and releases, the intensities and rests, the dissonances and harmonies of life—a "morphology of human sentience," to use Langer's phrase. [1] In more humble terms, I propose that spirituality has to do with sounding life before God. Because we live through time, music is perhaps our most natural medium for coming to terms with time, and attending to the transcendent elements in making sense of our temporality. Our lives, like music, have pitch, tempo, tone, release, dissonance, harmonic convergence, as we move through times of grief, delight, hope, anger, and joy. In short, music has this deep affinity to our spiritual temperament and desire. Our lives, like music, can be understood in remembering the passage through time. The order or sound is comprehended as we remember and re-configure the previously heard in light of the yet-to-be-heard. So, too, the deeper desires and yearnings of the human soul are not understood until a larger pattern emerges. Remembering the sound of voices of those we loved and lost to death is perhaps one of the startling examples of recapitulation and fresh re-understanding of that relationship as we move through time.

The foregoing reflections might be formulated in a second thesis: *Music is intimately related to the narrative quality of human experience, presenting our temporality in symbolic form, but always bodily perceived through the senses. Ritual contexts activate the formative and expressive power of sound with respect to the deep patterning of human affections.*

I now understand new depths of spirituality implied in St. John Chrysostom's remark: "The psalms which occurred just now in the office blended all voices together, and caused one single full harmonious chant to arise; young and old, rich and poor, women and men, slaves and free, all sang one single melody...together we make up a single choir in perfect equality of rights and of expression whereby earth imitates heaven" (*Homilies on the Psalms*).

When the Christian assembly gathers to sing in the context of worship, deep memory is required. The act of singing praise, lament, thanksgiving, and intercession to God goes beyond the surface of the words, and beyond the musical score. This event itself is metaphoric, parabolic, and symbolic. Singing/hearing music that expresses life before God confers a special dignity on our human desires. If the text and musical form are adequate to mystery, to suffering, and to the deeper range of human emotions, the human soul is available to the transfiguring grace of the divine life. This is the domain of liturgical spirituality. But such phenomena are also present in devotional and personal attentiveness to musical form—even to each distinctive sound. Gerard Manley Hopkins testified to this: each thing "Deals out that being indoors each one dwells." [2]

Spiritual formation and experience, by definition, take us beyond the obvious surfaces we perceive in hearing with the physical senses. Music is remarkably ephemeral, always passing away from us; yet it does seem to open "levels of the soul." The question of meaning in music hinges on the interaction, and the interanimation between order, sound, and the range of other senses—visual, kinetic, gestural—it conjoins. The circumstances under which something is first heard and then remembered lead to the deeper power of what music offers Christian life. Music is not therefore simply an ornament of something already understood, such as a text. Neither is music, in ritual and devotional contexts, an enhancement of something already fully determined by the text. Rather, music mediates multiple senses and the reception of religious significance precisely by crossing over to what is *not* heard. This begins with the human voice in primordial rituals with mother and child. Sounds convey bodily images; they have kinetic powers and evocative efficacy.

Even in hearing instruments or distinctive sounds such as the ringing of bells, we are called to attend to the interaction of all the elements of sound. Listening to another's voice, even in reading, requires vulnerability, acceptance, and expectancy. The tension is already there with respect to what is yet to be said and heard, and how this hearing will reconfigure the already sounded and heard. Thus it is no accident that we can "hear" in Bach, or in Mahler, or even in the simple deep folk tune a sense of height, depth, breadth, sharpness, softness, liquidity, marching, persistence, and free imagination. Sound implies spatial and kinesthetic orders. The deeper our hearing with imagination, the more these features emerge. Text, music, and bodily participation are fused together in ritual action. Thus music itself can become a gesture. Human speech is more than sound. Hence music shapes our capacities to envision, to come to a sense of being.

A final thesis emerges: *Synaesthesis (the engagement of several senses, triggered by one of them) is required for spiritual maturation. If we only take in the literal surface of what we hear in words and song, the awakening of the deeper dimensions of reality and of the soul are prevented.* When the singing and the hearing allow us to "taste and see," we come to "hear" more. The soul is awakened to a humanity stretched more deeply before the mystery and the glory of God. Worship can shape human beings in a growing maturity into the beauty and the holy fear of this temporal life. When sound in worship is adequate enough to engage the other "senses" in perception of the hidden glory and grace of divine self-giving, spiritual maturation is made possible. Something about "coming to our senses," about the mystery of existence, requires this. Something in us must be "sounded," just as we desire to hear and to speak of the divine-human polyphony.

Music can thus express the verbally inexpressible. For the tension between what we see and have not yet seen, what we hear and have not yet heard, is the pattern that a theological interpretation of life offers. Music has the power to engage more than the senses. Spiritual maturation into the deeper dimensions of what is real requires understanding something about the world and ourselves. This means that ordered sound must make connection with attitudes, beliefs, and sustained ways of viewing the world. Of course, not all music functions this way, nor is all music capable of shaping and expressing a "sense of the world." Yet, as we shall see, music both inside and outside the religious community—specifically the Christian traditions both East and West—may be integral to such a shaping and expressing that leads to a theological interpretation.

Don E. Saliers, _Music and Theology_

CHAPTER TWO

MUSIC AND THE BODY: CHRISTIAN AMBIVALENCE

Wherever human beings hear and encounter God, the consequences are poetic, visionary, metaphoric, and parabolic. The experience of God is received in sound and image—voices, instruments, the dance. Early on in Hebrew Scripture God calls: "Hear, O Israel..." (Deuteronomy 6:4), and this echoes throughout the centuries in Jewish liturgy. In the Christian Testament: "Faith comes by hearing, and hearing by the word of God" (Romans 10:17 *NKJV*). And the Psalms constantly evoke singing: "Sing to the LORD a new song" (Psalms 96 and 98). Luke can barely make it through two chapters of his gospel without breaking into song four times: the great canticles of Mary, of Zechariah, and of old Simeon commingle with the angels' spontaneous *Gloria in excelsis*. These songs, themselves echoing Hebrew prophets and psalms, have also been sung throughout the Christian church's history.

Despite all the tensions and temptations to the contrary, Christianity steadfastly remains a religion of the body and of song. From the beginning the gospel takes on human form and is proclaimed and celebrated in the human idioms of ordered

11

sound. This is why there is the impulse to sing with fresh accent the Word become flesh, and the hope that human beings will themselves live through the palpable, audible Word. This is why sound and spirituality go together—in order to sing and live the depths of life and death before God. "Out of the depths I cry to Thee" (*Aus tiefer Not*) sang Martin Luther, but also "A Mighty Fortress Is Our God" (*Ein feste Burg*).

In his insightful book, *Theology, Music and Time*, Jeremy Begbie explores how the study of music enriches theological thinking about basic Christian doctrines. He does this by focusing especially on music, time, and temporality. Music, he finds, so deeply engages time that it can provide the theologian with new "conceptual tools—ways of thinking, models, frameworks, metaphors—for exploring, clarifying and re-conceiving the dynamics of God's world and his ways with the world."[1] Early in his study he mentions four basic ways in which music is related to the extra-musical world. These four points set the stage for our initial discussion of music: it is a "living practice," it engages the physical world, it is "inescapably *bodily*," and it "has very strong connections with our *emotional life*."[2] I will expand on these basic points to set the stage here for chapters to follow.

First, music is a living practice. Musicians, and especially those who appreciate musical theory, recognize "formal" elements in ordered sound. Sound patterns can certainly be appreciated for their own intrinsic properties: melody, pitch, rhythm, tempo, harmony, formal structural patterns and the like. These are what could be called the "raw materials" available to all music making. Of course *how* these are put together to make music differs greatly from culture to culture, and from one historical period to another. A great deal of musical analysis and commentary has focused on how composers use the sonic materials. Yet the fundamental point is that music is a living practice of both making and hearing. Whatever the formal elements are, the "end product"—the music itself—gains its particular shape from the social and cultural context from which it arises. As Begbie observes, "Music always, to some extent, embodies social and cultural reality...no matter how autonomous with respect to intended function..."[3]

"Second, music-making and hearing arise from *an engagement with the distinctive configurations of the physical world we inhabit.*" [4] Isn't it interesting that the great majority of stories about origins contain acoustic images? A primary relationship with the world is found in the Genesis account: "God spoke, and it came to be." Joseph Gelineau, in reflecting on the human voice remarks: "The vast majority of cosmogonic stories [stories of cosmic creation] originating from the most diverse cultures call upon acoustic images to explain the origin of things… Everything happens as if the most intimate relationship which exists between a human being and [the creator] was first perceived…as being a resonant one: noise, sound, voice, music." [5] Perhaps this is because our first perceptions in the womb are acoustic: the mother's voice and heart beat, external sounds and rhythms. The voice thus becomes a primordial, prelinguistic force.

But every object in nature comes to sound something about itself: water, air, wood, stone, trees. More obviously, birds, insects, and animals of every description all tell us something of themselves by "sounding." In this way vibrations and sound waves take their character from features of the world of material and animate objects. Many composers and music-makers have explored the sounds of nature as part of their "language" of sound—most especially birdsong and weather, and more recently the sound of whales. Even when these features of music are absent, we are hearing ordered sound produced by air vibrating or passing through metal, the friction of bows on strings, and so on—the musical instruments themselves as "articulated" physical objects.

Third, music and its practice are "inescapably *bodily.*"[6] Whatever affects us spiritually or mentally also resonates within our bodies. This is especially true of rhythm and pulse. But all the features of ordered sound work through human senses to our understanding of our inhabited world. Ordered sound from "outside" our bodies resonates and evokes the music "inside" our bodies. The inner music is constituted by the very make-up of the human body: heartbeat, breathing, walking, and all the bodily gestures we learn and come to inhabit as a way of being in the world. Sound is sensual, yet as we shall note many times throughout our explorations, sound is also "interpreted." This requires a fusion of the senses and the intellect. Many dimensions of music exhibit this fusion: words and musical sounds, the passing of sound through time, the ability to hear a particular piece.

Finally, music is deeply connected with human emotional life. This leads us to the complex topic of just how ordered sound can express our emotions, much less actually form or shape how we experience ourselves and our world. This is crucial to tracing the way in which music and theological meaning are interrelated. Can music actually educate our emotional life, such that we may speak of a "joyful sense" or an "elegiac understanding" of the world? This in turn may shed light on how much religious and especially liturgical music both shapes and expresses our image of God. We shall see especially why music is indispensable to the theological significance of praise and lament.

These basic features of music account for the power of music to "move the soul" and to provide a way to shape and express religious experience and beliefs. Yet the very bodily and emotional power of music making and hearing has also created tensions for Christian theology and life. Return again to Augustine's famous passage in his *Confessions*. On the one hand he speaks of the role of music in his conversion: "The tears flowed from me when I heard your hymns and canticles, for the sweet singing of your Church moved me deeply. The music surged in my ears, truth seeped into my heart, and my feelings of devotion overflowed..." (*Confessions*, IX, 6). On the other hand he is worried that he will be carried away by the sensuous sounds and not pay attention to the sacred text of the psalms. He worries that the pleasures of music might lead him away from God and what God's Word speaks through the words (see the passage in *Confessions*, X.33, 9–50).

This ambivalence has a long theological history. Long before Augustine's personal testimony, the early church waged considerable polemics against certain forms of music, especially instrumental music and dancing. This was because of the dangerous association such music had with the immorality found surrounding Roman and Greek practices. The sensual qualities of music, including song, were deemed inappropriate for Christian worship and life, not so much because of a general denial of the body, but because of idolatry and the licentious potential of singing and playing in the theatre and pagan cults. So, for example, playing the lyre was associated with prostitution. The following passage from the fourth century indicates the force of this early polemic:

> In blowing on the tibia [pipes] they puff out their cheeks...they lead obscene songs...they raise a great din with the clapping of scabella [foot percussion]; under the influence of which a multitude of other lascivious souls abandon themselves to bizarre movements of the body. [7]

Augustine's quandary over the problem of music's sensuous distraction from God's Word introduces a basic philosophical conflict between body and spirit that will return, especially at the Protestant Reformation. Theological reflection about the nature and role of music often turns on how strongly the boundaries between the material, sensate, and spiritual worlds are drawn. Strong distinctions made between material and spiritual (body and soul) have consequences directly affecting the practice or suppression of music making within different Christian communities.

Perhaps the most dramatic instance of the Reformation era is found in the theology and practice of Ulrich Zwingli in Zurich. He was an accomplished musician; yet he shut the organs of the churches under his jurisdiction and did away with singing in the congregations. He knew how emotionally powerful music was and did not wish for it to be a sensual distraction from the "pure" Word of God. The church, in his view, should be separated from the entertainments of society and free from distraction. Reading and preaching were the "sounds" in worship, not instrumental or vocal music. Here the contrast between the world of spiritual reception of sacred texts and preaching and the world of sensual sound was deep. One side of Augustine's ambivalence triumphed. The irony is that Zwingli saw to it that musical training was provided for the children in their schools. How different this was from Martin Luther's practice and theology.

Albert Blackwell's *The Sacred in Music*[8] makes a compelling case for the "sacramentality" of music itself. Tracing two distinctive Christian sacramental traditions, he draws on both the central theological claim of the Incarnation and the contemplative tradition linking music to silence. Music is sacramental in that it contains the mystery of the inexpressible depth of reality, yet makes it audible and palpable to human sense. Both of these dimensions, he claims, mirror the very idea of the self-incarnation of the invisible God in the physical world of time and space, perceived by human senses. Thus music in its depth dimension bears the sacred mystery of God, who is transcendent spirit, made flesh.

Yet the very notion of music as potentially bearing the "sacred" suggests its contrast, the "profane." This leads again to the suspicion of music by Christian theology and toward a dichotomy of "sacred" and "secular." Both Protestant and Roman Catholic traditions have drawn lines, in various historical periods, between what is suitable to communicate theological matters, and what is unsuitable. This is seen in many attempts to prevent certain instruments and certain styles that had strong non-ecclesial or "sinful" associations from being used for Christian purposes. Calvin drew the line on textual grounds. Only the "simple and pure singing of the divine praises" is to be allowed, thus limiting what Reformed Christians should sing in church to the Psalms. However, this in turn delimited acceptable music settings. The paradox of Calvin's Geneva is that he employed some of the best tunesmiths in the French court traditions to compose many of the music settings of the Psalms. Some of these tunes are still cherished today for the quality of the tunes...and subsequently many hymns have been written for these durable lively tunes: *Rendez a Dieu, Donne Secours, Old Hundredth*, and many others.

We return to Augustine's deep attraction to music. He possesses a sensibility for what is beautiful, rooted in an inherited Platonic and neo-Platonic suspicion of physicality and the body, yet also steeped in the language of doxology born of the psalms and the affirmation of song. In his own theological discourse he becomes the poet, and the singer of deep images for God.

Whether intended or not, he cites the very sensible stuff of liturgical rites when he first denies that the love of God is "the body's
beauty" or "song's sweet melodies." Yet he says when he loves
God it is *something like* "light, sound, smell, food, and touch…"
He knows that some words are most deeply comprehended only
when they are sung. The sound (melodies) of those psalms in
Milan was intrinsic to how the words from God were received
deeply in his mind and soul.

There has been a persistent debate within Christianity about
words and forms of music. Controversies about what should be
sung about God and whether it should be accompanied by instruments or sung at all indicate the importance of thinking through
the relationships between theology and music. These controversies emerge precisely because music—played, sung, and heard—
remains both emotionally powerful and yet mysteriously
ephemeral, always passing away in linear time, yet always fusing
past, future, and present. This point is made strongly in Jeremy
Begbie's *Theology, Music and Time.* The controversies over the
theological significance of music and the Word of God also
emerge because music itself is subject to the tensions between the
material and the spiritual, since God is not a material object. The
consequences for the actual practice and valuation of music in
religious traditions are immense.

The role of music in Christian worship is thus subject to the
history of variable cultural artistic means. When Christianity was
presented to slaves of African descent in America, the "art" and
the aesthetics of song and ritual such as the "ring-shout" (a
tightly formed circle of worshipers simultaneously stamping out
rhythms and singing) emerged as part of the theological import
of that community. The way in which human suffering has
entered into the understanding of lament found in Scripture and
the language of prayer is theological matter of immense importance. Yet it is precisely music that aroused unholy physicality
and bodily engagement that other traditions, including later
African American "holiness" movements, found too "secular."
Since singing and instrumental playing have the power to evoke
the pathos of human life, the theological import of what and how

17

language about God and human life before God is sung becomes apparent. We will see this especially in the analysis of Christian hymns and song in chapter 4.

So it is that in the twentieth century, gospel music and jazz emerged as the peculiar fusion of African and European musical traditions in the Americas, and has made its way into liturgical and theological domains. As Alice Coltrane, creative musician and wife of saxophonist John Coltrane is reported to have said, "to play jazz *is* to worship—to be in church."

For now we must turn to the several tasks and forms of theology that are analogous to the multiple functions of music. What are the varieties of theological discourse that must be taken into account? How do these intersect, if they do, with multiple forms of musical expression that emerge as theological belief finds itself communicated in differing historical and cultural contexts?

THREE THEOLOGICAL AIMS AND MUSIC UNLIMITED

Howis music related to the aims of Christian theology? The question is much more complicated than we think at first. Much depends upon the theologian or theological tradition of which we ask such a question. "Theology" and "music" are general terms, so broad as to render problematic any simple theory of how they are related.

Music is, as Jeremy Begbie observes, a *practice*. More accurately, it is a set of related practices. One domain is *music making*—composing, performing a score, and improvising, to name three primary dimensions involved. A second domain of practice is *listening to music*—live in the concert hall, recorded music heard over numerous media, heard and sung in churches or schools. Each of these in turn shows different features. Listening, we often forget, is itself a disciplined practice; and listening to live performances also involves seeing the players, in a sense "seeing the production of sound." Furthermore, there are distinctions between instrumental music and vocal music, between wordless music and music combined with texts of various kinds. A third domain of music is *interpretation in the hearing* of music. Multiple types or genres of music—each with its distinctive characteristics—expand the horizon of our comparison even further. Each of these domains of practice is involved in any full account of what music is and does.

Theology, too, may be described as a set of practices—whether in writing or in speech, whether in the systematic setting forth of specific doctrines, or in hymns, sermons, prayers, or formulated creeds and confessions of faith. These are practices in language oriented to addressing and expressing God. Furthermore, there are multiple types of theological thinking. In Scripture itself we recognize narratives, parables, canticles, prophetic speech on the edge of poetry, and wisdom teachings, as well as the specific formulation of "doctrine"—what is to be believed about God and the world. We must begin with the fact that "music" and "theology" have multiple aims and functions. One must also wonder whether all "theology" must be confined to articulation in language; this is a question to which we will return.

If we begin with the broadest possible definitions of both music and theology, we may yet sketch some common elements. For example, music and theology each border on the inexpressible. Music has the power to move beyond mere sense experience. In its deepest forms, music often seems to express what language cannot say. It is a "language of the soul" made audible, but without words. Theology, on the other hand, must use language to the point of breaking when speaking of God. God is transcendent, but also immanent, both in Godself, and in relation to the world. Christian theology has always moved within the limits of human analogies: God is a "creator," but not simply like a human artist; God is "power," but not simply human power exaggerated; God is "love," but no mere projection of human love. God is not a space/time object, but is characteristically described by attributing characteristics of persons in space and time. God is often said not to be simply another being, but "being itself" or beyond being and existence.

Some forms of music evoke the unutterable—a sense of that which cannot be contained in the ordinary world of sense experience. Some philosophers have commented on the relationship between music and silence, a reality known only in and through ordered sound that propels the mind and heart beyond the knowable world. Music that sets specific biblical, liturgical, and doctrinal claims about God to melody and harmony is one place where theology and music explicitly converge. In certain pieces of music such as Vivaldi's "Gloria," or the choral conclusion of Beethoven's Ninth Symphony, both the music and the words evoke nearly inexpressible glory and joy. This hints at the fact that there may be a "theological music" and a "musical theology." These phrases will return in the final chapter.

The well-known hymn writer Brian Wren makes a convincing case for an expanded definition of theology. "Christian theology as reasoned enquiry hopes not merely to *express* and *convey* the faith called forth by God's self-disclosure…but to explore, discover, and know more about it. If there are [nonverbal] ways of exploring, discovering, and knowing…about God…they are *doing* theology, not merely expressing it, conveying it, or doing nontheological work with theological implications." [1]

Traditional definitions of theology, unlike music as such, are linguistically oriented. Theology is literally "words about God," even though mature theological discourse always acknowledges the limits of language. When we intend to speak of realities that transcend the world of space and time, we encounter the paradoxes of the unsayable and the inexpressible. This is why the venerable terms *beauty*, *goodness*, and *truth* still hover over us even in a "postmodern" world. Still, there might be modes of expression that move beyond such limits of language without denying that theology is primarily *logoi* (words) about *theos* (divinity). Among the arts, music provides hints at an answer, and some theologians have made this a theme in their writings. In addition to "visual theology" found in Christian art and iconography, is there not the possibility of an "acoustical" theology?

MARTIN LUTHER AND JOHANN SEBASTIAN BACH

It is well known that Martin Luther praised music as a wonderful gift from God. In his preface to the *Wittenberg Hymnal of*

1524, and in his preface to the 1538 collection, *Symphoniae iucundae* by Georg Rhau, he extols music as next to the very Word of God.

"I am so overwhelmed by the diversity and magnitude of (music's) virtues and benefits that I can find neither beginning nor end or method for my discourse...." Thus he focuses on the chief point: "that next to the Word of God, music deserves the highest praise."[2] Luther was convinced that a fundamental characteristic of faith in God was found in the fact that God is to be praised above all other reality. The Scriptures, according to Luther, constantly attest to this. Indeed, biblical faith is permeated by such praise. For Luther, the theological key to understanding the whole of Scripture was found in Jesus Christ. "After all, the gift of language combined with the gift of song was only given to man to let him know that he should praise God with both word and music, namely, by proclaiming [the Word of God] through music."[3]

The great sixteenth-century Reformer was also a musician. It can be claimed that the great eighteenth-century musician, Johann Sebastian Bach, was also a theologian, as Jaroslav Pelikan, Robin Leaver, and others have shown. For both Luther and Bach the communication and the reception of the Christian Gospel were unthinkable apart from music. So many of Bach's organ works and Sunday cantatas were based on Lutheran chorale tunes, thus musically proclaiming many of Luther's theological themes some two hundred years later. There could be no authentic Christian worship without the assembly singing praise and confessing their faith in song. At the same time, much of Bach's music—even without words—I contend, engages the performers and the listeners with theological content. To cite but one notable example, Bach's cantata *"Christ lag in Todesbanden"* (Christ lay in death's strong bonds) sets all the stanzas of Luther's original hymn, but with Bach's stunning harmonic and counterpoint. The result is a musical proclamation of the central mystery of the death and resurrection of Christ. This re-stating has, in the two-hundred-fifty intervening years, made Luther's Gospel claims alive across many Christian traditions—even in concert halls.

BACH AS MUSICAL THEOLOGIAN

Johann Sebastian Bach (1685–1750) is acknowledged as one of the greatest of all composers. This is not simply because of the vast quantity of compositions, nor only because of the memorable quality of his music. Rather, Bach's greatness is attributable to the manner in which he sums up an enormous range of developments before his time, and anticipates so much future music. In a word, his music is generative in both directions. In listening to his music one comes to appreciate so much of the multiple traditions he draws upon, but one also hears anticipations of so much yet to come in Western music. While there has been scholarly debate over the role of faith and theology in Bach's musical productivity, there can be no doubt about the theological legacy he actually leaves to posterity.

The Bach cantatas were performed every Sunday in the two major churches in Leipzig from 1723 to well beyond Bach's death in 1750. If we think of the "sacred" cantatas as being written very specifically for the church's liturgical year, it follows that those cantatas are a form of theology set to music. Not all of his cantatas were "sacred" in this narrow sense, however. He composed in the cantata form for birthdays, royal court events, and anniversaries. But upon closer examination, Bach moved so easily between "sacred" and "secular" compositions that we should not try to summarize his achievement by drawing an overly sharp contrast between these categories. There is musical borrowing both ways across the whole range of Bach's work.

Jaroslav Pelikan observed, "a substantial percentage of the music in parts 1 through 5 of the *Christmas Oratorio* was in fact recycled from three secular cantatas (BWV 213–15), composed during the autumns of 1733 and 1734." [4] Yet in so doing, Bach surrounds the borrowed elements with new musical material. In setting biblical narratives and images concerning the nativity of Jesus Christ how he uses the instruments and the qualities of the borrowed materials are altered because of the new subjects.

Pelikan asks, "What happens to the distinction between the 'sacred' and the 'secular' Bach in light of his concrete practice as a composer?" [5] It was "the privilege of the composer's spirit to praise God" (in the Mass in B Minor's "*Osanna in excelsi*") even "when he was not composing for the church...The performance of any God-pleasing vocation was the service of God." [6] This accounts for the theological impulse behind Bach signing many of his works *soli Deo Gloriam*—"to God alone be glory"!

KARL BARTH AND HANS KUNG ON MOZART

No discussion of theology and music would be complete without at least a brief mention of Wolfgang Amadeus Mozart (1756–1791). His music has attracted two most remarkable theologians, Karl Barth and Hans Kung, one Protestant and the other Roman Catholic. Each of these theologians has discerned in the whole range of Mozart's music, both "sacred" and "secular," a profound religious and theological impulse. Karl Barth remarked that if he ever got to heaven, he would "first of all seek out Mozart and only then inquire after Augustine, St. Thomas, Luther, Calvin, and Schleiermacher." [7] He obviously thought that in Mozart's music, more than in any other place, he discerned an "art of playing" that presupposes a "childlike awareness of the essence or center—as also the beginning and the end—of all things." [8] Even more Barth heard in the music of Mozart a way of understanding how the dark and the light of the created order are found together, with the dark never threatening the light of God's love for creation.

Hans Kung, reminding Barth that Mozart was a Roman Catholic, argues that religious categories are needed to describe and interpret Mozart's musical achievement. He turns his attention specifically to the *Coronation Mass*, exegeting Mozart's musical insights into the *Gloria*, *Kyrie*, *Credo*, *Sanctus*, and *Agnus Dei*. Yet in the end, both Kung and Barth celebrate Mozart's musical/theological "Yes" of salvation amid all the negativities of human existence. Kung cites Barth's remarkable statement about the *Coronation Mass* as musical theology:

> Herein is the strangely exciting but at the same time calming quality of his music: it evidently comes from on high, where (since everything is known there) the right and the left of existence and therefore its joy and sorrow, good and evil, life and death, are experienced in their reality but also in their limitation. [9]

Such appreciations of Mozart, I contend, indicate the possibility of "hearing" and "overhearing" implicit and explicit theological soundings in the very musical structures and the full achievement in composers such as Bach and Mozart. What we must still ask, later in our exploration, is what the theological trajectories and implications are of very different kinds of music— music not bound so closely to biblical and liturgical traditions.

MULTIPLE THEOLOGICAL GENRES AND AIMS

For now, we turn back to the varieties of aims and types within the broad domain of "theological discourse." Readers may be familiar with terms that name different types of theology: systematic, historical, philosophical, pastoral, moral, and liturgical, to name several. Each of these types is a distinguishable academic field of inquiry. For example, historical theology studies the origin and development of Christian thought, whereas dogmatic theology, such as found in Karl Barth's *Church Dogmatics*, characteristically exposits the logic and content of classical doctrines of the Christian faith. Pastoral theology is concerned with the theological interpretations of Christian practice that constitute the church's and believers' concrete lives in context. Liturgical theology seeks to make explicit the theology formed and expressed in the worship of God. Alexander Schmemann, the twentieth-century Russian Orthodox theologian, initiated a vital recovery of this form of theology in his early *Introduction to Liturgical*

Theology. But this recovery points back to much earlier ways in which the substance of theology was found in prayer and worship. Bishop Ignatii Brianchaninov was fond of saying, "If you pray truly...you *are* a theologian." [10] Who can doubt that the poetry of the fourth-century Syrian Christian writer Saint Ephrem—known as the "harp of the Holy Spirit"—is lyric theology? Listen to a sample of his famous "Homiletical Rhythms on the Nativity":

> Glory to that Voice which became Body,
>   and to the Word of the High One which became Flesh!
> Hear Him also, O ears, and see Him, O eyes,
>
> ....
> Ye members and senses give praise unto Him...
> Mary bare the silent Babe, while in Him were hidden all tongues! [11]

These examples tell us that not all theological discourse and modes of reasoning can simply be lumped together. Yet all forms of theological reflection aim at faithful discourse about God, the world, and humanity. Our concern is with the possibility of a "musical theology" and a "theology of music." Liturgical theology has a strong interest in how hymns, psalms, canticles, and the people's acclamations in the liturgy are a *theological* as well as musical practice. I consider this form of theology a central discipline in thinking about music.

Both philosophical and systematic theology have a special interest in aesthetics. They are interested in music as a human temporal art. In both cases, music may be claimed to provide analogies and models for thinking about such key notions as time, transcendence, and eternity. Jeremy Begbie's provocative book, *Theology, Music and Time*, is an attempt to show how music gives theology new resources, especially for thinking about the Holy Spirit. Both the concern with music as a theological/ liturgical practice and music as a revelatory art are part of our concern here.

In sum, there are multiple forms of theological discourse, each with its distinctive purpose and rhetorical style. Music, on the other hand, is not on the page, but is always live "ordered sound." Yet it too has multiple forms and functions in human life. In our present situation, music is found in "dizzying variety." Jan Michael Joncas has expressed this well:

> The musical world is . . . fragmented and diversified, ranging in academic art composition from the quasi-total determinacy of computer-generated scores to the quasi-total indeterminacy of composers like John Cage with serialists, minimalists, resurgent romantics, and performance artists vieing [sic] for attention. The popular music world has likewise fragmented into various niches of rock, rap, jazz, musicals, country, and world music with dizzyingly changeable subcategories constantly being generated and marketed. Genuine folk music continues to be sung by some U.S. communities, but it is more frequently represented by professional folk singers who operate in an entertainment market. [12]

Indeed such "dizzying variety" is part of what we must take into account. More important, how music actually functions in people's lives is immensely varied. Theologians may be tempted to think first of "classical" or "high art" music as presenting the most likely candidates for theological interpretation. This has certainly been true of most writing about hymns, anthems, and other forms of church music. I honor this point in the following analyses of hymnody. But theological relevance, much less particular theological content, cannot be confined to the "art music" traditions. The folk music and "spirituals" traditions are equally our concern, as is the very act of singing for justice and freedom, as we will see in chapter 5.

It is enough here to point toward the intimate connection between music and the act of public worship, beginning with the more liturgical uses of music.

MUSIC AND CHRISTIAN WORSHIP

Paragraph 112 of *The Constitution on the Sacred Liturgy* comments on music in Christian liturgy. Musical tradition is integral to the worship of God because "as sacred melody united to words, it forms a necessary or integral part of the...liturgy." [13] In this sense music that is wedded to liturgical actions and to the prayers of the assembly is never an ornament or a mere accompaniment to worship. Rather, music is intrinsic to the acts of proclaiming, praying, and enacting the mystery of the divine-human encounter. This is one of the most obvious relationships between music and theology.

Questions about music in worship are thus questions about the nature of the Church at worship. Assessments of the liturgical use of music are not simply musical; assessing the adequacy of music in praise of God is both aesthetic and theological. The musical idiom conveys a great deal about how the community conceives of God. Acoustic images reflect theological imagination at work. When the quality of music is grandiose or pompous, the projected image of God may contain more of the self-image of the worshiping community than the community realizes. When the quality of music is pleasant and folksy, the projected image of God may be strong on intimacy and ease, but lacking in awe or mystery. Yet, as we shall see, much depends upon the language used to address God or to describe God's relation to the world and to human beings. Gregorian chant is simple in one sense, but not without mystery. The same may be said for melodies from folk traditions...such as are found in Appalachian traditions or in the Spirituals. So we must attend to the wedding of text and tune, and to the way in which the assembly actually sings—what musicians refer to as the "performance practice" of the words set to music.

Can music alone, without words, be theologically significant? For anyone who regards theology as always strictly a matter of verbal claims to truth, the immediate answer is no. Should what we mean by "theological discourse" be so restricted? In our experience of music in worship, most will say that while music as such does not make "truth claims," it always enhances what the texts say and mean. But even more often we have experienced how a particular melody or musical setting seems to "embody" or "sound like" the truth when we take it to heart. The hearing of the melody itself or the music without the words still evokes the power of the story or the particular text. Can we say that on particular occasions it is the music that carries far more than the "feeling" or the association with words? There are times when we stand in awe and wonder by virtue of the voice or the instruments giving us access to the holy, to a sense of awe and wonder at "being present" to God and the assembly.

But might there be particular occasions when a piece of music carries with it more than association, and more than the arousal of feeling—music without words as revelatory of transcendence? What do we make of "revelatory" experiences with the music of Christian worship?

If this is to be possible, then the notion of theological significance must be broadened to include more than theology as statements about the divine life. Perhaps there is something about the ancient conception of theology as prayer, as liturgy, as poetry and song that we must recover today.

Think of an occasion in which music you were hearing overwhelmed you with feeling. You may think of listening to a car radio and suddenly having a song evoke a person you love, or a place you had deep associations with—a seacoast, a city street, the house you grew up in. Or you may think of a concert when you first heard an orchestra play Stravinsky's "Rite of Spring," or Tchaikovsky's "1812 Overture." It was as though a new world opened to you through the ordered sounds. Yet again, you may remember singing a certain piece in a high school or church choir that, whenever you hear it again, opens up something in your soul because you have sung those words to that melody. It is somehow inscribed in the memory your body retains despite the years.

Any and all of these experiences can teach us something of the power of music. There is something of a mystery here. First, that something as passing and seemingly insubstantial as sound can stay with us over time may strike us as hard to explain. But in the second place, the very fact that music seems to lie so close to the way we have actually experienced a person or a place is mysterious. Further on we may come to marvel at the way music is produced by human breath blowing into an instrument, or by human hands and fingers striking a drum or a keyboard or bowing a stringed instrument. However we humans come to the awareness of it, the mystery of music itself is a wonder.

Music has powers beyond language to describe. Why can't we describe the sound of an oboe or a cello? Of course we can speak of the music as "sad," "happy," "rollicking," or "haunting." But that is to name its effect on the hearer. We often try to form analogies to describe the sound: "That sounds like many birds singing" or "That trumpet makes a strong, golden sound" or "Her voice was like velvet, or like crystal."

How can music evoke images in the mind? Some music is deliberately composed to imitate birds, or the rolling tides of the sea, as in Debussy's "*La Mer*." Other music is clearly meant for marching, as with a military band, or meant for dancing as in country fiddling. Other music sounds like warfare or like a sweeping vista of mountains, forests and rivers, pines and fountains, as in Ottorino Respeghi's brilliant "Pines and Foundations of Rome." We are not surprised that music creates and evokes visual images. What is puzzling is how music uses ordered sound to do so. Yet we know that the shape and pulse and pitch of music echoes something of the very way we experience our world and our lives. Music often imitates and evokes how we "picture" being in the presence of things, or how we experience seeing.

All of these general features of music combine to make us wonder at its very existence and power in human life—both in individual consciousness and in the role it plays in societies and the range of human communities that make and enjoy music. Any study of the relationships between music and religious belief, much less efforts to articulate particular theological truths must begin by acknowledging the power and, yes, the mystery of music. Abraham Heschel, the great twentieth-century rabbi poet, observes that "Religious music is an attempt to convey that which is within our reach but beyond our grasp."[14] We must attend both to the qualities of music and to the way in which music affects the listener.

There is a connection between music and human speaking that is a necessary part of this story. Young children in every known culture first learn their native language by listening to and imitating the sound of words . . . to the tones of voices. Some languages are much more explicitly "tonal" than others. That is, the sounds of the words are intrinsic to the meanings of the words. In speaking and learning to understand one another, we come to learn the "music" of the sound of language as well.

A child first learns to imitate the "music" of words and especially the patterns of sounds as spoken by parents and others. This is why, for example, small children love to have someone read to them. Even though they do not understand the words, they recognize the rhythms, the pitch, and the tone of voice that accompanies and gives sense to the reading. Storytelling is even more dramatic because it also involves reading the facial and bodily expressions of the storyteller. These ordinary facts about learning a language illuminate a connection between music and theological thinking.[15]

Because of theologians such as Luther, Barth, and Schleiermacher (on the Protestant side), a persistent strand in the Patristic thinkers, as well as subsequent Eastern Orthodox and Roman Catholic theologians, it is possible to reconnect the multiform practices of theology with the nature and power of music that moves toward transcendence.

Theology Sung: Hymns, Psalms, and Spiritual Songs

When I want to know someone's conception of God I ask what his or her favorite hymns are. Of course the list of hymns reflects what a person has grown up with, and reveals something of the denominational and musical sensibility of church experience. Alongside what these hymn choices reveal about the social conditions for having learned to sing the words, I find that hymns correlate closely with what people believe about God, Jesus, the Church, divine grace, and what the Christian life should be.

This chapter explores some key examples of hymns that continue to shape what we could call the "operational theology" of both individuals and communities of faith. The letter to the Colossians admonishes the community to teach the wisdom of Christ, reinforced by singing the faith. "Let the word of Christ dwell in you richly; teach and admonish one another in all wisdom; and with gratitude in your hearts sing psalms, hymns, and spiritual songs to God" (3:16). Such hymns, psalms, and spiritual songs are the very language of thanksgiving to God. While this does not give us a formal typology of song, it clearly indicates the role of music in communicating central Christian claims. Even more, this call for singing faith is directed at giving a *theological shape* to the living of a particular way of life. A parallel passage found in the letter to the church at Ephesus accents the emotional depth of the practice of communal song. "Be filled with the Spirit, as you sing psalms and hymns and spiritual songs among yourselves, singing and making melody to the Lord in your hearts, giving thanks to God the Father at all times and for everything in the name of our Lord Jesus Christ" (5:18b-20).

We might call this a theological melody. To use the older Latin phrase, singing faith is the *cantus firmus* of the whole Christian way of life. From the beginning of the Christian movement and the earlier communities the faith was learned and expressed, in part, through song. Four major aspects of these musical practices compose a pattern of sung theology: praise and thanksgiving, petitionary prayer, proclamation, and narration of the mighty acts of God. Tracing these four aspects through several historical periods will illustrate the range and power of a sung theology.

The praise of God is born in the acknowledgment that God is the creator of heaven and earth, and the source of goodness and mercy. In this sense Christian theology cannot be understood apart from the Psalms and the heightened speech of praise and thanksgiving that appears in Hebrew scripture. The psalms are both song and prayer, characteristically addressed to God. When Psalm 103 sings, "Bless the LORD, O my soul, and all that is within me, bless his holy name" the song ascribes to God healing and forgiveness, redemption by God's love and mercy, renewing human beings, and working justice for all who are oppressed. That is, we learn who God is in the very act of praising and blessing. Psalm 104 proceeds from the opening *berakah* ("bless the LORD") to sing the whole wonder of creation and the marvelous being of God.

But song is also offered as prayer to God in all its modes. The psalms are both poetry and prayer, and they form a kind of grammar of praise to God from which Christian hymnody takes its principal themes. Augustine's simple definition of a hymn is revealing: a hymn is "praise to God in song." Obviously the history of hymns we know today shows a much broader set of themes, but this initial grammar of praise and thanksgiving to God is central. It was a dominant theological element in the earliest hymns, both in Greek and in Latin.

The early hymns, filled with light and glory, proclaimed who God is and, offered at sunrise and sunset, truths about God's relationship with the creation and with humanity. There is a strong use of scriptural images that express the way God is conceived. So God's Word in this sense was not only preached, but also sung. Hence much of Christian hymnody is exegetical—it interprets Scripture. From earliest times, Scripture lessons were sung and chanted—also an inheritance from Jewish liturgical practice.

In the New Testament various kinds of musical forms are mentioned. Even the doxologies that conclude some of the Pauline and other letters were known in the liturgy of the earliest communities. This is indeed how the worshipers are to teach Christ to one another. Clearly these musical/acoustical elements are theological, and not merely psychological aids to feeling. That is, in the act of singing or reciting in heightened speech, theological meaning was communicated.

That there is theology in hymn texts is obvious. What is less obvious is what kind of theology this may be said to be. Even less obvious is how musical settings contribute to the theological sense of the text. One way to think of these issues is to regard hymns (text and tune together) as "lyrical theology." This means, as we saw in chapter 3, that we must give "theology" a broader definition than is found in most standard textbook accounts. I propose that "lyrical theology" be placed alongside dogmatic, philosophical, and systematic theology. It could even be argued that more formal notions of giving an ordered account of the doctrines of the Christian faith depend upon what is prayed and sung and proclaimed. [1] The formal language of reasoned reflection on Christian doctrine requires the primary theological "language" of sound that both forms and expresses faith in local assemblies. This, I propose, always involves music and related forms of ordered sound.

Throughout the long history of Christian song, we can trace ever shifting theological accents. Many hymn texts are born in theological controversy. For example, many Protestants claim "Faith of Our Fathers" as one of theirs. But F. W. Faber, (1814–1863) originally wrote the words as an Irish Catholic protest in England: "Mary's prayers shall win our country back to thee..." Using the same melody, Protestants omitted such words and made it speak another theology. But the great majority of hymns we now sing from the whole history speak to the human situation in light of the doxological worship of God, or, as in the case of the Social Gospel of the early twentieth century, of a prophetic word to the conditions of suffering.

Gail Ramshaw's *Words That Sing* explores ways in which hymn texts from many centuries "sing" doctrine and spirituality. She writes, "The church's collection of hymns is an ecumenical treasure. In the hymn-singing traditions, hymns become central to the people's piety. Hymns are the primary way that the liturgical year and theological imagery are appropriated by the laity." [2] It is the sung imagery that becomes part of the embodied memory of the church and of individuals.

Within her survey of the major periods of church hymnody, she cites Isaac Watts's remarkable hymn "Go Worship at Emmanuel's Feet" that employs fourteen images for Christ that convey the adoration and praise of Emmanuel:

> Is he a Tree? The world receives
> salvation from his healing leaves.
> Is he a Door? I'll enter in;
> behold the pastures large and green.
> Is he a Star? He breaks the night,
> piercing the shades with dawning light. [3]

Hymns are theological miniatures. If you ask ordinary worshipers what has shaped their theological convictions about God, Jesus, Church, and the Christian life, they will most likely refer to hymns. Hymns are, especially in Protestant traditions, the bearers of the images that are both theological content and experiential patterns of faith and affection. What is often not noticed, however, is how the music itself makes connections between texts and carries the memory patterns of particular theological themes and images. One fascinating example is how a well-wrought tune can carry multiple texts and offer a connecting link. How many words can be sung to a great tune?

Here are three that can be sung to John Goss's fine nineteenth-century tune, *Lauda Anima*. The original text by Henry F. Lyte, "Praise, My Soul, the King of Heaven," is itself a paraphrase of Psalm 103. In 1980, William Boyd Grove wrote "God, whose love is reigning o'er us, source of all, the ending true," which the tune animates strongly. More recently, from the Iona Community in Scotland, come John Bell's words accenting a contemporary set of themes, praising the creator of the world who is the God of justice, love, and peace. His hymn text stresses the Christ who "feeds the hungry, frees the captive, finds the lost / Heals the sick, upsets religion / fearless both of fate and cost." Here he uses the shape and rhythm of the melody to good effect.[4]

In singing this bold new text, I find that the tune also evokes, as part of the depth of these new words, the psalm, the nineteenth- and the earlier twentieth-century words as well. Only music can do that. This power of music to make present images and narratives in ever-new contexts has been part of what composers have done in larger works, both instrumental and vocal.

All three of these hymns are about God as Trinitarian life. All three are doxological, with increasing additions of sub-themes. The music sets all three texts well; the tune has a strong forward-moving line with considerable vitality. None of the lines are the same, though the meter of 8.7.8.7.8.7 keeps an accentual pattern that brings out key words. In the first two texts, the word "Alleluia!" is doubled exactly at the high point of the melody. In the third hymn ("Praise with Joy...") the climax of the tune takes the contemporary word "celebrate" in three of the stanzas, with the final stanza proclaiming "This the world shall see reflected: God is One and One-in-Three."

In each case the theological sense of the text gathers round what is the musical high point as well. This wedding of text and tune brings forth the theological content in ways that a lesser melody cannot. If we read the text aloud, we can grasp how well suited this particular tune is to all three of the texts. This is why, in a recent hymn collection, *The Upper Room Worshipbook*, the editors chose to group all three under the tune *Lauda Anima*.

One of the strongest and most explicit theological justice hymns is Albert Bayly's "What Does the Lord Require?" It begins with the ringing question asked by the prophet Micah (6:8). The answer? "Do justice, love mercy, walk humbly with your God." The text hovers closely to the words of Scripture. When the musical setting is added, the text deepens. The melodic tune by Erik Routley creates urgency. It is plaintive, strong, and unexpected. Even as I have become familiar with the tune, it still works its way. The harmonic shift intensifies the force of the question, setting up a tension that only the answer can resolve. The music contains a dramatic octave drop just before the last phrase occurs. But the music doesn't allow the singers to fall back into presumption. The music itself, I contend, sustains the tension found in Micah. Even when the answer is given, the question of living it—embodying the justice, the mercy, and the humility—remains. It is as if the hymn propels the singers toward the inevitable confrontation with ourselves and with how we are to live. The music echoes Micah's prophetic challenge: shall we, *can we*, live this way? And the theological point is that God demands this form of life from us. [5]

At the same time, different musical settings of the same text will highlight and bring forward different nuances of meaning. A good example is found in one of the most widely sung hymns of the late twentieth century, "When in Our Music God Is Glorified." Written by the British Methodist poet Fred Pratt Green (1903–2000) it is held in special affection by church musicians. Because of its lyrical strength and the intentional focus on the music itself, it is a worthy epigram for this chapter.

When in our music God is glorified,
And adoration leaves no room for pride,

It is as though the whole creation cried:
Alleluia, alleluia, alleluia!

It concludes with a ringing admonition:

Let ev'ry instrument be tuned for praise;
Let all rejoice who have a voice to raise;
And may God give us faith to sing always:
Alleluia, alleluia, alleluia! [6]

Each stanza carries a strong theological affirmation that issues in a triple "alleluia" of praise. Thus it is both a sung act of acknowledging God, and a self-reflective theological affirmation of the central meaning of worship. This much can be known by simply reading the text. But when it is sung to a stirring musical setting such as the tunes *Engelberg* or *Fredericktown*, [7] the words sound what they refer to. The fusion of text and tune is more than the text alone. There is an "affective knowledge" of the words that comes with the music and the conjoining of voices in the act of praise. I find the concluding single "alleluia" especially strong in the tune *Engelberg*, rising in thirds to a joyous climax.

Of course there are hymns that contain both poor poetry and impoverished theology. This means that we should distinguish between descriptive and normative accounts of hymns. Not every example can be said to convey adequate Christian teachings or doctrine. In fact, many hymns are not at all concerned with theological doctrines. Many hymns focus more on the feeling states of believers, or on admonishing the assembly to action. Though even in these cases, there is usually an implicit theological claim in the background.

Obviously one can study the theological content of these texts quite apart from the musical setting. My point is that, studying how persons come to depict God in these texts is shaped by the singing practice itself. This means that various points of description and ascription of the divine will be accentuated, or even diminished, by the singing practices. Once a hymn text is released musically into the bloodstream of a congregation's repertoire, it plays a deeply formative role in the shared theology of the assembly. Even more significantly, hymns are part of the process of coming-to-believe. More than once we hear of how the very act of singing attracts the searching soul. In her book *Traveling Mercies*, Anne Lamott tells of being drawn by authentic gospel music coming from a "ramshackle building with a cross on top." It drew her back to something deep and missing in her life at the time. "Somehow," she recalls, "the singing wore down all the boundaries and distinctions that kept me so isolated. Sitting there, standing with them to sing, sometimes so shaky…that I felt like I might tip over, I felt bigger than myself, like I was being taken care of, tricked into coming back to life." [8]

For all this, there is still a difference between singing theological beliefs in hymns, anthems, and more extended musical forms, and the work of systematic inquiry into the meaning of theological claims, with the use of philosophical reasoning. [9] The point of this chapter has been to invite a reconsideration of the primary role that sung theology—as prayer, proclamation, and imaginative exploration of religious belief—has in religious communities. While sung theology is not intended as conceptual or analytic, it nevertheless can make profound contributions to our theological experience and understanding. As Brian Wren reminds us, "precisely because it has few words to play with, one way in which a hymn can do theology is to state, pithily and vividly, theological viewpoints whose claims are argued elsewhere, or to frame praise, thanksgiving, longing, lament, trust, commitment, and other God-centered responses based on such viewpoints." [10]

In every historical period, synagogues and churches have discovered in singing their faith "new dimensions in the world of sound," as Fred Pratt Green's "When in Our Music God Is Glorified" expresses it. The music sounds and intensifies the images, the metaphors, and the narrative elements of sacred texts. But when the music itself is strong and durable, it becomes part of the body's memory of the words, thus creating permanent access to lyrical theology. It is the musical setting that accumulates to itself associations of time, place, persons, and encounters which ever after are contained in the singing. Thus it is that hymn and anthem texts, cantata and oratorio settings of Scripture come to be inscribed deep within human lives. From time to time we rediscover theological truths about God, the world, and human existence by simply hearing a melody or the sound of a voice, or an instrumental version of a well-known hymn.

This astounding truth is powerfully put in a stanza from Brian Wren's recent hymn, "Give Thanks for Music-Making Art":

> With music, moving on through time
> in sequences of sound,
> We show and tell God's story-line
> of how the lost are found:
> The old, unfolding covenant
> of justice righting wrong
> resounds through word and sacrament,
> and leads the people's song. [11]

SINGING AS POLITICAL ACT: THEOLOGICAL SOUNDINGS OF JUSTICE

There are so many reasons to sing, and so many seasons of singing among human societies. People sing for pleasure, people sing for and about love, people sing their lamentations and cry out their sorrows. The entire range of human experience has found its way into song. There is also a strong strand of singing for justice in many communities and cultures, particularly in times and circumstances of oppression; but especially when the need arises to voice what the God of justice demands. This leads us to the threshold of this chapter: *singing as a political act and its theological implications*.

Human groups have often used music, and especially public singing, for political ends, for good or for ill. On the one hand the American Civil Rights Movement, on the other, the Nazi *Jugendleid*, youth marching for the Third Reich. In the greatest propaganda film of all time, *Triumph of the Will*, Leni Riefenstahl used the music of Richard Wagner to accompany images of *Der Fuehrer* coming through the clouds to earth in a plane to land in triumph. There was surely a political theology in visual and acoustic images.

Suppose we define "political act" as a specific human engagement that aims to reshape and affect the *polis*. Of course there are engagements with the political order that bring adversarial and even destructive chains of events, as in the example I have just cited. We do not have time in this book to develop the larger story of the "good" and "ill" of music used as political means. Rather, I am interested in exploring how singing itself can be considered an engagement with the political order that calls the *polis* to its own best being and practices—that is, singing that aims at restoring the commonweal of social and civic life. Singing for justice in the face of oppression thus becomes a political act of resistance to idols, and a prophetic call for the transformation of the order of things. Here music itself becomes a theologically relevant action. In particular, I am concerned here with Christian song and its cross over into social and political song.

THE POWER OF BIBLICAL CANTICLES

Let's begin with one of the most powerful songs in Christian scripture that, while the church often sings it innocently or piously, contains a subversive if not radical call for justice. It is the *Magnificat*—the song of Mary. Isn't it interesting that Luke cannot get through the first two chapters of his gospel without breaking into song four times? Mary, Zachariah, old Simeon, and the angels' *gloria in excelsis* punctuate and permeate Luke's narrative. In the *Magnificat* Luke's account of the annunciation of the nativity of Jesus—the promised Messianic birth—breaks out into a song that, if I may say so, still lies in wait for the Christian tradition to catch up with. As the seventeenth-century poet John Donne observed, "it contracts the immensities." Here is forever the connection between the divine act of incarnation and a witness for social justice. To sing with Mary is to sing God's justice.

Mary's great prophetic outburst begins in wonderment and doxology: "My soul magnifies the Lord, and my spirit rejoices in God my Savior." Behind the words of this canticle we recognize its source in the more ancient Song of Hannah (1 Samuel). Both the prophetess Hannah's prayer and Mary's song are proclamatory and dangerous. They are dangerous to the powers of this world that hold dominion over the poor. No wonder Paul Westermeyer claims: "It should not surprise us that the *Magnificat* is deeply imbedded in the church's liturgies nor that dictators find it so offensive."[1]
Listen again to the familiar words:

> He has shown strength with his arm;
>   he has scattered the proud in the thoughts of their hearts.
> He has brought down the powerful from their thrones,
>   and lifted up the lowly;
> he has filled the hungry with good things,
>   and sent the rich away empty. (Luke 2:51-53)

This promise is to all future generations: that God will continue to be this way...

Therefore, beware monarchs and oppressors of every age! Mary's song is waiting to be taken to heart and to the very thrones of power. It is an innocently disguised political gesture in song—and potentially subversive.

Yet Mary's canticle belongs to a much longer history of songs of praise that protest. The heightened speech of the prophets and especially of the Psalms form the great stream of tradition from which the *Magnificat* and the other Lukan canticles spring.

The Hebrew psalms are permeated with the cry for justice. Singing the Psalter to a righteous and holy God (33:5; 97:2; et al.) calls for accountability—on the part of both the singers and of God. Again and again God is called upon to "defend my cause" (Psalm 9:4). Psalm 72:2 calls upon God (through the king) to "judge your people with righteousness, / and your poor with justice." "The LORD works vindication and justice for all who are oppressed" sings Psalm 103:6. Praise and doxology commingled with lament...but both together keep circling around the themes of justice and protest against injustice.

Walter Brueggemann speaks of Israel's praise as "revolutionary in its world-making...raw in its power...the nations are invited to a new world with a public ethic rooted in and normed by the tales of nameless peasants, widows, and orphans. It is enough to make trees sing and fields clap and floods rejoice and barren women laugh and liberated slaves dance and angels sing."[2]

Our Puritan and Presbyterian forebears mainly sang the Psalter, as Calvin insisted. One can only imagine the impact on their sense of duty and their "fear of the Lord" upon hearing and singing the seventeenth-century translation of Psalm 82 by Tate and Brady:

> 1   God in the great assembly stands,
>   where his impartial eye
>   In state surveys the earthly gods,
>   And does their judgments try.
> 2,3 How dare ye then unjustly judge
>   or be to sinners kind?
>   Defend the orphans and the poor;
>   let such your justice find.
> 4   Protect the humble helpless man,
>   reduc'd to deep distress;
>   And let not him become a prey
>   to such as would oppress.[3]

To the Psalms we must add most of the canticles from Hebrew scripture, beginning with the songs of triumph over those who enslaved Israel, as in the songs of Miriam and Moses in Exodus 15. The heightened prophetic speech we hear in the poetic songs of second Isaiah (chapters 60–63) creates a pulse and rhythm of justice throughout the prophetic literature, carrying over in the songs and hymns of Christian faith, as we shall see.

MORE THAN THE CHURCH'S SONG

But the biblical songs that unsettle the powerful and cry for the oppressed are not confined to the church alone. This theme of song justice to God carries over into what we sometimes call the "secular" world (though the whole dichotomy between the "sacred" world of church song and the "secular" world of singing is quite misleading).

If the biblical connection between singing and the press for human justice outside of church was ever in doubt, read some pages from a book by Guy and Candie Carawan called *Voices from the Mountains*. I had occasion to speak at length with them at the Highlander Folk Center in Tennessee. This was the place where many of the leaders and participants of the Civil Rights Movement and other freedom struggles have received training and support since the 1930s. *Voices from the Mountains* tells the story of what the Carawans recorded of the songs from Appalachia from the 1940s through the 1970s.

This music comes out of struggle, pain, and courage in the face of enormous economic and social hardships. We might call music that sustained hope in difficult times a "survival art." But more to the point: these songs were of protest and affirmation rooted in a religious and moral tradition born of Christian faith. Many of these songs originated in protest against working conditions and the rape of the land that accompanied coal mining. A singer named Sarah Ogan Gunning sang the mournful "Dreadful mem'ries, how they linger" to the old tune "Precious Memories": "...they ever flood my soul. / How the workers and their children died from hunger and from cold." The song goes on to speak of thugs hired by management, and violence against the workers and their families. As the wife and daughter of coal miners, Sarah saw this suffering up close, including her own child's death by starvation. No wonder the song cries: "Really, friends, it doesn't matter, whether you are black or white. / The only way you'll ever change things is to fight and fight and fight." [4] This is not the church's devotion, nor the concert hall—this is raw stuff from the earth and from the heart of a people who yearn to be free of economic slavery. But it is a cry that transforms yearning into action. Songs like that "move the soul" and hence the social body. This is the sound of political theology.

In Emory University's Cannon Chapel in 1981, we brought in a group of singers among whom was a ninety-year-old ex–coal miner named Nimrod Workman. He was particularly outraged at the extent of black lung disease among the miners. He would take a traditional melody, known in the mountains—so often a religious song—and would adapt its words into a cry for justice.

One example is to the old tune "Don't You Want to Go" ("to heaven" in the original). The music is a plaintive melody, carrying the older evangelical religious fervor about heaven. But Nimrod Workman's new words—and hence the "new song"—names the realities of suffering and oppression here on earth. The singing of it was an act aimed at social transformation. Each verse begins with a haunting invitation, "Don't you want to go to that land where I go?" and proceeds, in verse after verse, to offer "that land" as heavenly alternative to the earthly evils that plague the miners: "Be no strip mining in that land. . ."—no low wages . . . no exploitation . . . no black lung . . . no politicians. The song asks again and again, "Don't you want to go?"[5]

But these songs, having emerged out of older gospel traditions, remind us of a still more venerable singing tradition in which political resistance and protest are always just beneath the surface: the Spirituals.

SPIRITUALS AND THEOLOGICAL–POLITICAL SOUNDINGS

The Spirituals, of course, are the great body of music born of suffering created by the enslavement of some for the economic gain of others. This was suffering that we can barely comprehend . . . families deliberately torn apart and human beings regarded as chattel, less than human. Such oppression was a crucible; out of which was forged not only remarkable survival, but lamentation and subversive song, as James Cone and others have taught us.[6] When the slaves sang "Go Down, Moses, Way Down in Egypt's Land," the evocation of Moses the Liberator was clearly tied to a cry for freedom—and for a new Moses to do away with their oppression. When the strains of "Steal Away to Jesus" sounded, it was both a piety focused on consolation in their Lord and a code for escape, especially through the Underground Railway.

The one place for those under slavery to speak freely in lamentation and in yearning was in the religious gatherings. So in worship in the "hush harbors" (meeting in the "brush arbors") the cry to God was sounded. Consequently the Spirituals carried forward the theology of Jesus' identification with the oppressed. "Nobody knows the troubles I've seen," or "Woke up this morning with my mind stayed on Jesus," and countless others sounded a whole theology of God's identification with the enslaved.

Not the words only, but the power of the melodies and the way the whole body of the community sang the words, sounded the deep religious passion of such a theology.

Out of this remarkable singing tradition were born the civil rights songs themselves: "Keep Your Hand on the Plow, Hold on, Hold On!" "Woke Up This Morning with My Mind Stayed on Freedom," "Ain't Gonna Let Nobody Turn Me 'Round." These songs and this singing carried the workers into the teeth of dogs and the assaults of police blackjacks and high-pressure fire hoses. As noted in the workers' protest songs of the 1930s and 40s, the civil rights music was constantly adapting new words to older melodies, often naming those who were the persecutors. When one traditional song was first adapted by the movement in Albany, Georgia, the names of the chief of police and the mayor were included: "Ain't gonna let Chief Pritchett turn me 'round...Ain't gonna let Mayor Kelly turn me 'round."

One of the most significant musical gatherings of the entire Civil Rights Movement took place in Atlanta in May 1964. The Sing for Freedom workshop, sponsored by the Highlander Folk School, SCLC (Southern Christian Leadership Conference), and SNCC (Student Nonviolent Coordinating Committee), brought together the musical protest traditions of the North and the South. Musicians and activists came from all over, listening and sharing songs from their own local communities. Present were great singers and songwriters who were already in the movement in the South: Fannie Lou Hamer, Bernice Reagon (later of "Sweet Honey in the Rock"), Cordell Reagon, and Betty Mae Fikes. From the North came well-known folk singers Phil Ochs, Tom Paxton, and Theodore Bikel.

Sing for Freedom may have looked and felt like a festival, but it was clearly also an event of great political importance in the civil rights struggle. Guy and Candie Carawan, activists and folk-lorists, told me that hearing the old songs and the history was rev-elatory for some of the young freedom fighters. [7] Imagine what it must have been to be with the Georgia Sea Island Singers; with Doc Reese from the Texas prison system; Ed Young, the cane fife player from Mississippi; and the Moving Star Hall Singers from Johns Island, South Carolina. Fresh songs emerged in this cre-ative cauldron, as unexpected new verses were added to older melodies. Joshua Dunson's memoir of those four days in Atlanta, entitled *Freedom in the Air*, describes the overwhelming power of the gathering:

> In the song "This Little Light of Mine," five, six, seven or eight Leaders would introduce verses that were from their communi-ties. Betty Mae Fikes of Selma, Alabama, whose voice is steel, set the pace with the clapping of her hands: "Up and I'm bleed-ing, / I'm going to let it shine," singing despite the violence done to her. Doc Reese sang: "Voting for my freedom, I'm going to let it shine. Let it shine. Let it shine." There was that tremendous impact that only occurs when 50 or 60 song lead-ers bring their voices and clapping together in thunderbolts of song for 20, 25 minutes of letting your whole body explode into song. [8]

The older songs, "Negro songs," commingled with newer free-dom songs. This great variety led to clashes of opinion, for many of the younger black radicals did not want to hear the old mem-ory of the slaves of an oppressive theology. But in the end, the connection between the older music and words and the emerg-ing, more "political" songs was made. What had been preserved in the deep religious tradition under slavery was precisely a cry for freedom. This was the religious and theological taproot of the relevant new songs of protest for change, motivation, and hope-driven energies of the movement.

It should then be no surprise that twenty-five years later, the anti-apartheid movement in South Africa was also carried on the force of song as political act: "Siyahamba! / We Are Marching in the Light of God." Siyahamba! Born in the scriptural song for justice and transformation of the world, the great river of politically relevant theology is carried in a wide range of places.

BACK TO THE CHURCH: HYMNS OF SOCIAL VISION

As an early teenager I remember being moved by a well-known hymn, "The Voice of God Is Calling." The sturdy melody fused with the words: "I hear my people crying in cot and mine and slum…" It asked those who sang it: "Who will go to help my people in their need?" I'm not sure I understood what "cot" meant, but the hymn captured my imagination. This is what the church is called to do. Another hymn, with its great melody in a minor key (most church people prefer "happy major keys"), fairly shouted its prayer: "O God of Earth and Altar, bow down and hear our cry." It sang of "earthly powers" faltering, and that "people drift and die." This was my first awareness of a period of great hymn writing that called for action. Much later I learned of the hymns of the Social Gospel that stirred a whole generation to social vision.

The church, the polite and well-ordered community of Jesus Christ, often worries that singing some of these songs will violate boundaries between religious faith and politics! But what began in the Hebrew Scriptures and carried on into Christian song and hymns cannot be stopped. Hymns that sing of radical justice of God ought to agitate and disturb us. Many recent hymns combine strong melodic, rhythmic, and harmonic elements with strong words as in Fred Pratt Green's "When the Church of Jesus

Shuts Its Outer Door" that critiques a complacent church. Other settings combine musical understatement to explosive texts, such as Shirley Erena Murray's "Peace Child," set to Bernadette Farrell's haunting lullaby.[9]

But in addition to protest and resistance songs there are those songs that simply open up the "new creation" liberationist themes without a hint of stridency. One powerful example is the hymn *Cuando El Pobre*: "When the poor ones who have nothing shared with strangers... Then we know that God still goes the way with us."[10] It is liberation theology set to song that disarms us.

OUTSIDE THE CHURCH THE BEAT GOES ON

If we listen closely, the song that calls us to remember the poor and the captives of this world and its suffering can be found in unlikely places. When Joan Baez sang "Blowin' in the Wind" or Bob Dylan sang "The Times They Are A Changin'" to an earlier generation, the political winds were blowing. When later generations of folk and alternative rock singers carry this forward, we hear it again in new accents. So, for example, the Indigo Girls' song "Our Deliverance" sings of soldiers' blood drying in the desert, "can we not fertilize the land with something else?" We are still looking for our deliverance, but it "has already been sent" and "love will find us, just like it has before."[11] This is protest and it is hope. Many contemporary rock groups such as U2 or Public Enemy ("Don't Believe the Hype") sing prophetic words and a musical call to responsibility in the world.

In 1988, a year before the Berlin Wall fell, Maestro Robert Shaw directed the Atlanta Symphony Orchestra and Chorus in East Berlin, performing Beethoven's Ninth Symphony. When the final chorus had finished singing Schiller's great ode to freedom and brotherhood, the audience was stunned. Shaw shook his fist in the air as the auditorium burst into wild applause. I cannot help but think that Beethoven and those musicians contributed to the fall of that infamous wall of separation and death.

Let us say that one of our most profound human responsibilities is speaking truth to power, especially when power is corrupt. Music that sings this way has been and remains an instrument of vision and social transformation—a powerful religious and political impulse has been unleashed in this world.

Human communities must continually rediscover the stretch between praise and prophecy, between lamentation and righteous indignation. Singing as a political act needs its counterpoint in memory, praise, and lament. In the remarkable story of the French village of Le Chambon in the years of the Second World War, the villagers hid more than a thousand Jews right under the noses of the Nazis stationed in the village. Years later one of the children saved by the village returned to do a television essay and interview. He asked Madame Trocme, the widow of the Huguenot pastor: "Why did you do this? How did you do this?" She replied simply: "Because this is what Christians are supposed to do." Disarming. But behind this enormous political act I think lies a body of Huguenot hymns that sing of the Huguenot martyrs over hundreds of years. Those hymns had their effect over a long period to produce a courageous character in a whole people.

Whenever and wherever we sing of God's future, there remains the possibility of our singing being intrinsically a political act. In this sense all faithful praise and lament carries the seeds of recognizing the huge gap between the IS and the OUGHT TO BE of this world. Of course, this can be perverted or even distracted by our singing. As Westermeyer observes,

> Hymnody and its context can all be an empty shell, ingrown, self-centered, and even evil. Such a perversion is the ever-present danger. We dare not forget Amos's "Thus says the Lord: I hate your assemblies, take away the noise of your songs, I will not listen to the melody of your harps, but let justice roll down." There are times when such words need to be uttered, which is why the worshiping community against whom they are directed has itself preserved them. [12]

But I say more than this. I say this is why the song of the psalms and of justice sung in prayer and worship cannot be confined to the church. Indeed, perhaps in our time, we know much more of its depth outside the rooms of worship than inside! But just about the time I say this, I suddenly realize how much recent hymnody has relearned this. The crossovers are many and powerful.

We should also know that when we hear singing as a political act outside the church, we are reminded of the origins of that singing. In the Scriptures, the journey of people of faith who sang out on behalf of the world as well as of themselves, captured in song a theological truth. So the history of suffering is inscribed and performed in human communities of breath and heartbeat and hand clapping, and in great choirs with great instruments in accompaniment. This great river of humanity is conjoined before the God who gave us the gift to sing, and the gift to cry out, and the will to be faithful to God's own intended OUGHT TO BE for the world.

CHAPTER SIX

BEYOND "SACRED" AND "SECULAR"

It is easy to take music for granted. We live in a music-saturated culture. Television and radio offer a jungle of musical snippets to sell everything from medication to cars, from food and drink to insurance. Music accompanies shopping, aerobics, and nearly every human activity that needs "mood" or background sound. Popular music—from country to hip-hop—is instantly available on iPods, portable CDs, radio and TV, and now on cell phones. Millions of people still go to hear live music in rock concerts, recitals, and other performances. There are still those who gather to sing and make music together—usually in churches, synagogues, and schools, or around a campfire. It is easy to think of all commercial popular music as "secular," having nothing to do with religion, much less with theology; and all the music heard in churches and synagogues as "sacred." This is a common sense view of things.

But against this easy labeling, I contend that it is not so easy to draw hard and fast distinctions between the sacred and secular in music. In fact, these terms themselves have shifted meaning in relation to one another in light of complex cross-influences of music over the centuries. Various Christian traditions have attempted to draw strict boundaries between music suitable for sacred use and music that is not suitable. These have often been stated as matters of theology. Certain music is "unsuitable" for the praise of God. Yet the contrast between "secular" and "sacred" music shifts with ever-changing social and cultural contexts. We are again, in North American cultural contexts, in a time of debate and controversy over these terms.

In the early church the unsuitable music was rejected because of its close association with theatre, with Roman bacchanalia, or with pagan cultic religions. [1] While the New Testament and the first-century church did not have a polemic, by the time of the third and fourth centuries, Christian worship and life had encountered a much stronger set of musical forces within multiple cultural contexts. Thus the development of Christian hymnody and chanting came into competition with such unsuitable musical idioms. The polemics continued on into subsequent periods.

John of Salisbury strongly criticized the development of two- and three-part music in the twelfth century. "Music sullies the Divine Service, for in the very sight of God, in the sacred recesses of the sanctuary itself, the singers attempt, with the lewdness of a lascivious singing voice and a singularly foppish manner, to feminize all their spellbound little followers with the girlish way they render the notes and end the phrases." [2] The irony is that three- and four-part polyphony soon became accepted as established "sacred music" in monasteries and cathedrals in Europe.

In every historical period, new forms of music emerge that are incorporated into the music of the churches and synagogues. More elaborate musical developments in the Medieval period eventually deposited themselves in the great achievements of the Renaissance, and eventually in the musical vocabulary of Johann Sebastian Bach. Yet there were conflicts of sensibility all along the way. The critique, and even the vehement rejection, of musical styles occurred both in church music and in the evolving music of the period outside the church as well. The traditions of "sacred music" show constant attempts to draw boundaries at the very same time that religious communities were borrowing musical developments from the larger culture. Yet this "borrowing" was always modified by the religious tradition.

A clear contrast between sacred and secular appears in the famous *motu propriu* (1903) of Pius X (*Tra li solectitudini*), which sought to define "true sacred music." Plainsong and polyphony (!) were given priority, as were organs over all other instruments. But drawing strict boundaries is not only done by the so-called "liturgical" churches of the Roman Catholic, Anglican, or Lutheran traditions. Holiness and Pentecostal traditions at one time forbade certain kinds of rhythms, harmonies, and styles of singing, as we will see below. Many conservative Protestant churches, once scandalized by "fiddling," saw the eventual rise and use of bluegrass music as a common idiom for singing Gospel songs and hymns.

Every religious tradition, and indeed every human culture, inherits a set of acoustic images and convictions that define what makes music "sacred." Within Judaism and Christianity this is an especially complex history. When Pius X's *motu propriu* of 1903 declared Gregorian chant to be the supremely sacred music for the liturgy, with Renaissance polyphony nearly equal, he was reflecting the ideals of the nineteenth-century Roman Catholic tradition. For it was during the nineteenth century that the vigorous recovery of chant (by the Benedictines) and polyphonic music (in the Caecelian movements) was taking place. Within Judaism, the Enlightenment in Germany and Austria brought a new sensibility to the synagogue; consequently the music for prayer and sacred texts became heavily influenced by western music theory and compositional and performance styles.

Readers are perhaps too familiar with the clashes of sensibility in contemporary churches. So much so, that many despair of having any set of norms governing music suitable to prayer and enactment of public worship. As one wit is reported to have said in the late 1960s, following the Second Vatican Council: "Suppress the Latin and you get *glossalalia!*" More recently, popular and commercial song and music styles have become central to so-called contemporary Christian worship services. "Sacred" is often thought of as "traditional" and therefore not relevant to how a particular generation approaches religion and the expression of faith. Beneath our often well-defined concepts of what is "sacred" and what is "secular" is a continual history of changes. The very notion of "sacred sound" is thus demythologized into another genre of "social construction."

While liturgical music is only a sub-set of the larger notion of "sacred music" it nonetheless provides a key to issues of music and theology. There are certainly differences in how people experience a sense of transcendence, or of sheer beauty, or of such vitality and energy that they associate it with the effect of the Holy Spirit enlivening the world.

Nowhere is this more evident than in recent African American church traditions—and others influenced by them—that employ commercial "Gospel" music.

A recent book by Jerma Jackson, *Singing in My Soul,*[3] traces the emergence of Black Gospel music out of previously regarded "secular" and worldly music. At the heart of her narrative is the role of women musicians, born in the holiness and Pentecostal churches. The story of Sister Rosetta Tharpe is a touchstone to the tensions between the "sanctified" church music traditions and the emerging commercial music that placed black musicians in the world of "gospel superstars." Music in the holiness and Pentecostal church traditions was bodily expressive. This produced a style of solo singing with instrumental accompaniment that laid the groundwork for the "gospel music" sound outside the sacred church traditions. As Jackson observes, "Even as church members eschewed changes in fashion, they embraced the flood of new, affordable musical instruments created by industrial production."[4] So the use of drums, guitars, tambourines, brass instruments, and vocal production with "blue" notes and ecstatic improvisations emerged in the 30s and 40s. Later such gospel music became "secularized." Yet, as Jackson suggests, there are elements in those very musical idioms that still evoke the religious origins.

In the more "classical" musical traditions, recent music by Arvo Part and John Tavener has returned to much earlier sacred musical forms, including both Western and Eastern Christian chant forms. Both believers and non-believers have come to appreciate their music in concert and recital halls, and have been drawn by what one friend of mine calls their sense of "sacrality" in sound. More recently the extraordinary setting of the Passion story of Mark (*La Pasión Según San Marcos*) by the Argentinean composer Osvaldo Golijov has drawn rave reviews for his powerful "secular" multicultural approach to the sacred text of the earliest gospel. In this remarkable concert piece one hears the story interpreted through a complex layering of cultural aesthetics— Jewish, Christian, Latin American, and a fusion of instrumentation and vocal sounds.

We now bring a new set of listening ears, a new attentiveness to the *intrinsic* qualities and capabilities of music that show the ambiguity of all such easy sacred/secular distinctions. Not that we must do away with the terms "sacred" and "secular," though it may also be important to contrast "sacral" with "profane." For surely it is still the case that what moves us most deeply (rather than merely entertains us) has both contemplative and prophetic powers, and is visionary, carrying with it a "sense" of life and world. This is hinted at when music is heard so deeply that "you are the music while the music lasts" to paraphrase T. S. Eliot's line.

With these brief hints we can now acknowledge the musical "crossovers" that no longer surprise us: Benny Goodman playing Mozart and "Stompin' at the Savoy"; Yo Yo Ma offering both the Bach unaccompanied cello sonatas and the sensuous tango. Renee Fleming singing with great skill glorious arias as well as ballads and the blues. Even more to the point, the twentieth century emergence of jazz and folk settings of the Mass, and the compositional and performance styles used by serious church music drawn from musical theatre and cross-cultural sources.

These point to a tendency in the late twentieth century toward a wide musical eclecticism. Churches and synagogues live in such a time of musical range, and are confronted with the task of making judgments about musical suitability for worship. The awareness of what is called "global" music has complicated and enriched the picture enormously, since much new music that has been welcomed by many churches, both Protestant and Roman Catholic, has religious origins in other cultures. Recently, popular songs and hymns from Africa, Latin and South America, the Pacific Rim, and Asia have found their way into the repertoire of North American Christian churches. This situation contributes to yet another reconsideration of what is "sacred" and what is "secular."

With all this confusing richness of access to a wide variety of musical types and styles, it is still the case that some music astonishes the listener, and creates a state of consciousness that cannot be found in the ubiquitous music that surrounds our daily lives. So it is that, even the musically untrained still find Mahler's *Resurrection Symphony*, a late Beethoven string quartet, Haydn's *Creation*, or Britten's *Rejoice in the Lamb* to be music that moves us toward religious and spiritual considerations, if not explicitly theological awareness.

Other music, because of its life-origin, charges words so deeply into us that we are changed: "We Shall Overcome" from the Civil Rights Movement; "Siyahamba" from the anti-apartheid movement in South Africa; or any of the enduring African American spirituals. Music and song in times of great pain and disorientation illuminate the truth for generations long after. Hearing and singing some music makes us understand ourselves and our world better—even when there are not explicitly theological texts.

We need not work with dichotomies between "sacred" and "secular" music as such. Perhaps we need much more to attend to what can be called the "sacrality" or even the "sacramentality" of music wherever and whenever we are moved out of ourselves and our habitual, common-sense world. This can occur when we cease to be interested in music only for entertainment or "background" purposes, and begin to pay attention to how music points toward the deep elemental facts of our existence. Music may point, for example, to our mortality, our capacity for love and suffering, or to a sense of mystery beyond the commonplace or the mere appearance of things. This might be indeed music evoking and sustaining in us restlessness for God, and for a redeemed world. The late Maestro Robert Shaw used to say that great music always requires two things (in addition to musical skill): a sense of mystery and a sense of suffering.

Consider four proposals that may guide us back toward sacrality in attending to what music is capable of evoking and sustaining within and among us.

1. Music confers upon human words addressed to the divine its originating silence and mystery.
2. Music is intimately related to the narrative quality of human experience—presenting us our temporality in sensual, bodily-perceived images. The sound of the human voice is primordial, yet always linking sound to what is most intimately and deeply human.
3. Music can approach the inexpressible—awakening the deeper dimensions of what is most valuable and real, and opening the soul itself.
4. The theological import of music is not confined to "high art" traditions, but comes in the form of folk traditions, which often carry the "life connection" that theology shaped by the doctrines of creation, incarnation, and redemption requires.

The act of singing is a deeply human act, found in every culture. This is so because singing activates things that seem so central to human life itself: bodily, emotional, intellectual, and moral animation. To sing requires breath, physical production of sound, emotional resonance, uses of the mind, and characteristically collaborative patterns of listening and participation.

If these things are so, then the act of singing to God is a deeply theological act, which may also be a political act, as we explored in the previous chapter. Sung praise and praise to God is more than intellectual understanding and assent to claims about God. Singing *enacts* the praise, thanksgiving, and blessing. Singing also *enacts* sorrow, anger, lament, and the questioning of God. We see this especially in the Hebrew psalms. While singing may also teach or inform faith about theological doctrine, its primary drive is to form and express faith in the realities about which worshiping congregations sing.

Thus when a Christian assembly sings the doxology, or a communion lyric such as "You satisfy the hungry heart with gifts of finest wheat"[5] it uses the language of address. The music is addressed to God, whatever it may wish to proclaim *about* God, or about the singers themselves.

Many specific religious texts have found their way into the concert arena, and into popular music as well. I am convinced that there are spiritual dimensions to be discovered in all kinds of music. Yet some music simply lacks the qualities of sound and the evocative power to awaken matters of spirituality. Not *all* music is either implicitly or explicitly "theological." So much depends upon the uses to which music is put, and what the listener is trained and constrained to listen for. What concerns us now is the implicit theological force of music that can bear both a sense of life—the mystery of our suffering and joy—and hints of God-with-us. Now we are in a position to see that emotional feelings conveyed by music are more than merely passing sensations. Could it be that we cannot understand the world theologically except by being formed in certain emotions and dispositions that music engenders?

Today, under the inevitable impact of recorded music, cross-cultural influences, and ecumenical sharing, we face an increasingly contested marketplace of available music. We cannot simply rely on older definitions or inherited categories. The question of specific qualities, objectively given in music, must be raised. Features of human receptivity as well as ritual and non-ritual functions of music are crucial to the search for relationships between music and theology today. How shall we listen and become attentive to what music can give to theological reflection?

When performing musicians read a musical score, they enter into a complex process of "reading" and "interpreting." An accomplished singer or pianist, for example, soon learns that the music is not on the page. The music, as we have already noted, is the living sound that is produced by singing or by playing the instrument in accordance with the notated "map" on the page. The music is the tonal forms that sound the air and are taken in by the ear. This means that what lies beneath the surface of the

notes is more powerful than the notes on the page. The page cannot interpret itself.

Yet what is produced in sound requires knowing the score. Or,
in the case of improvised music, knowing the possibilities of
melody, harmonic structures, and dynamic ranges available on
the particular instrument. Above all, in music both played from
a score and improvised without a score, the sound depends upon
the imagination of the performer...how should this sound, and
how do certain skills with the instrument produce particular
"interpretations"?

I'm thinking just now of jazz artists such as pianists Art Tatum,
Bill Evans, Dave Brubeck, Oscar Peterson, or the sax of John
Coltrane. In listening to them one comes to appreciate the aston-
ishing possibilities that ballads such as "Over the Rainbow" or
"Lost Out Under the Stars" can "speak."

But I am also thinking of the great French organists who
improvised enormously complex pieces based on plainchant
melodies, or from themes suggested by hymnody, or submitted
beforehand in concerts. Could it be that music offers, in both its
structures and its improvisations, an image of how life may be
lived? Always in time; always with the task of listening for the
music that will give us the clues to meaning; always the need to
learn how to lament, to praise, to rejoice, to love, and to judge
truthfully. When we ask of ourselves to find the melody and the
polyphony of themes and the rhythms that allow us to flourish
and to come to terms with this mortal life's poignancy and
beauty—then music takes us close to the concerns of theology.

Theologians have spoken of how art can lead us toward God.
Often this takes the form of metaphorical expressions: "beneath
the surface" or "beyond the words or gestures." Friedrich
Schleiermacher spoke of music and the "feeling of absolute
dependence," Paul Tillich spoke of the "depth dimension" of reality revealed to a certain way of attending to the world and to
human experience. Karl Rahner spoke of the "self-transcending"
character of certain human experiences; and even Karl Barth,
who avoided attributing much to human experience, could speak
of "Glory" as a graced acknowledgment and attentiveness of the

world. It is no accident that he listened to the music of Mozart every day of his adult life.

There are some analogies between faith and the experience of music that are central to our inquiry. I think it not inappropriate to speak of the "mystery" of what is hidden in music, just as we might speak of the mystery of what "eye has not seen, nor ear heard." Yet music remains within the domain of the senses while pointing to a potential unity of the intellect, the emotions, and our openness to the mystery of being in the world. This is a not a matter of more "information" but a matter of hearing and seeing in depth what is already before us in the music. This is the synaes-thetic matrix of which we spoke in chapter 1. It is a matter of receptivity to the "pattern of life" and the mystery of being—and being "attuned"—in so perceiving the world.

CHAPTER SEVEN

LISTENING FOR THE MUSIC OF HEAVEN AND EARTH

M usic and the hearing of it are not two different things, but are simultaneously part of what is meant by music having religious or theological significance. Certain forms of music "sound" primary features of our sense of being alive. Hear again Joseph Gelineau's reflections on the human voice: "The vast majority of cosmogonic stories originating from the most diverse cultures call upon acoustic images to explain the origin of things.... Everything happens as if the most intimate relationship which exists between a human being and [the creator] was first received by [human beings] as being a resonant one: noise, sound, voice, music." [1] Some music can evoke the sense of hearing the originating energies of life, and can "sound" a sense of coming to rest in the whole of the created order of things. The opening measures of Joseph Haydn's "Creation" come to mind; or in a completely different way, Darius Milhaud's "Le Creation du Monde."

Sound itself reveals something about all physical objects. The sound of the human voice, however, carries with it a central characteristic of what it is to be human—the awareness and the ability

to "speak" the world of objects. Speaking and singing are tonal
sense-making instruments of communication. Human perception, reception, and the expression of being in the world are all
found in the singing voice. It is one thing to cry out in anguish
or ecstasy, and another to sound the anguish or ecstasy in language that moves musically between persons. So music emerges
both from the encounter with the sound of things and events in
the created order and from the resonance or *attunement* that the
human voice can replicate and represent. As Gelineau says,
"Music as art would not have such a wide range of connotations
nor such a strong capacity to stimulate if it was not rooted in the
totality of the cosmos and the human body, if it was not allied so
closely to the mind and to the Spirit." [2]

As many philosophers and theologians have observed, music is
close to "spirit"—a non-material medium of receiving and conveying a sense of the world. In our deepest attentiveness and
encounters with certain forms of music, we are opened to a depth
of awareness; a feeling about life that words alone cannot give.
This is why we must pay attention to what the music on its own
elicits, conveys, and evokes about being alive. This is in part to
call attention to how music is able to encode how life "feels" as
we live through time. Paying attention to what music elicits and
evokes also opens up two interrelated powers: music without
words as having theological import, and the fusion of words and
music forms to carry us beyond what the words alone signify. Both
of these "powers" of music are related human experiences of time
and space.

Life itself is filled with our own passage through time. Human
beings are temporal and our experience is of seemingly unrelieved
temporality. All things change and we are sometimes overwhelmed by the sense of the perishing. Music captures this
ephemeral aspect of our existence. On the one hand we can use
music to *distract* us from mortality and the passage of time; on the
other music can also *awaken* the poignancy of our passage
through time. Considered rightly, music can also offer insights on
how theologians may re-think questions of time, temporality, and
the experience of grace. [3]

LISTENING

The interwoven patterns of music and theological concerns in human lives also ask something of us as listeners. Here I wish to contrast being "consumers" of music and becoming attentive listeners. It is too easy in a music-saturated culture to think that hearing is something quite passive. All we have to do is turn on the switch (radio, television, CD player, or iPod) and let the music be our sonic background. Music in its deeper range cannot be confined to background sound, try as we might to keep it that way—a kind of constant accompaniment to our hours, or as accepted entertainment. Because music has power to speak and to reveal more than the mere organization of sound, we ask: what can music require and even demand of us as hearers? It is to the "listening practices" we must turn in order to appreciate how important "active receptivity" is to recognizing and experiencing theological dimensions of music.

The act of listening to music is crucial to the theological significance of music, with or without sacred texts. For "hearing" music as the bearer of theological import requires not only a "musical ear," as we say, but also a sensibility for hearing music *as* revelatory.

It should not surprise us that some persons "take in" more about certain kinds of music than do others. The difference is, in an obvious sense, a matter of training. The training of the ear for hearing is both the discipline of "paying attention" and the discipline of recognizing what one hears. Of course this can readily lead to subjectivism; reducing the music only to what the listening subject is capable of taking in. Yet, unless we mark the role of attentiveness and recognition of spiritual and theological "content" of certain music, we miss a crucial point: the deeper the mutuality of the musical patterns and qualities, the more complex are the capacities required for hearing.

In referring to Dietrich Bonhoeffer, the German Christian theologian who was executed just before the liberation of the death camps in 1945, Jeremy Begbie asks: "When Bonhoeffer, living out his last months in prison, finds that he has music constantly on his mind, and that he resorts to the language of polyphony to do his theology, is this not because his life has been significantly shaped by music, both as a listener and as a practicing musician of considerable skill?"[4] Bonhoeffer was trained musically. Moreover he could hear in music a many-voiced language of hope and beauty, even in the midst of prison. But the greatest feature of his notion of the "polyphony of life" is how he brought his whole life experience to music, and how he could allow the music to interpret his whole life.

For the attentive listener there are times in which the very notion of the subject and the musical "object" is overcome. The music so pervades us that we understand the hope and the fear, the terror and the beauty of life. Not everyone is pressed to the extreme, nor is everyone as capable of bringing the fullness of life to music as was Bonhoeffer. Yet I think what makes music profoundly religious and/or theological is the reciprocity of sound and life through time. Here again one thinks of the sound of the human voice speaking and singing what human beings live through in time. I am convinced that certain musical experiences give us the sense of the music transformed into the very melody and rhythm of how life is experienced. Such music can be very simple as in a child's lullaby or folk melody played on a dulcimer or song flute; but it may also be a great symphonic theme, or a complex polyphonic piece sung by a choir.

Our experiences of certain musical forms and of specific musical works will deepen our theological perception over time, provided we bring as much of life as possible to those works. This is why, for example, the very melody of "Amazing Grace" evokes deep stirrings toward God, even among professedly secular people.[5] As a church organist I cannot count the number of times I have accompanied this in a funeral service. It is also why, in hearing works such as Bach's *B-Minor Mass*, or Haydn's *Creation*, or Benjamin Britten's *War Requiem* over many years, they come to play an important theological role in our experience as well as in our thinking about God, the world, and human destiny. Whether in African American spirituals, hymns, oratorios, or opera, we are in the presence of theologically significant works of the human spirit. The question is whether we have the ears to hear. What such religious or theological hearing requires, of course, is more than the physical ears, or even good intellectual "ears"—this requires listening with the ears of the heart.

In this sense we could liken deep hearing of music to the "seeing" of religious icons. Something more than the physical eye gazing upon an image is required. Seeing an icon requires also a trained mind and sensibility to "read" the icon in such a way that the person is gazed upon by the image. This involves the "eyes of the heart" open to receiving a divine communication. In like manner, music can be regarded as offering acoustical icons. Just as the theological significance of the icon can be set aside to appreciate the image as an artifact of human making, so music can be simply admired for its structure, its elements, and for how it gives us pleasure. But the theological import of music requires a kind of active receptivity that is more akin to prayer, to contemplation, and to attending the world with a sense of wonder and awe.

The astonishing thing before us is this: yet to be composed, performed, and heard is music that engages us with the suffering and the mystery, the joy and the glory of being human in a God-given created order. And from time to time we will perceive and be challenged to think out the spiritual and theological implications of such music. Even now a new generation of composers is exploring musical "languages" that evoke mystery and transcendence, some rediscovering ancient texts and musical forms.

For those in Christian communities, and with friends from other traditions, we do well to heed language from sacred writings that reminds us: "What eye has not seen, nor ear heard, is prepared for those who love God." When, for you, the song of earth and the music of heaven meet, you will understand what these chapters have tried to say about music and theology.

THEOLOGY AS MORE THAN WORDS ABOUT GOD

Several years ago I was teaching a setting of Psalm 95 to prepare for an occasion of Morning Prayer. The refrain carried the words, "Listen today for God's voice, harden no heart, / Harden no heart." The music setting was by the gifted Australian composer Christopher Willcock, S.J. The congregation was learning to sing a repeated *ostinato* while the singers sang the text of the psalm, layering the music over the congregation and the instrumental accompaniment. After some time the congregation began to breathe the repeated words *as* music, sensing that the prayer of the psalm was being "prayed through them" by the music.

This reminded me of a question once asked by Frank Burch Brown in a paper dealing with Mozart. He asked: Can music voice what God wants us to hear? The answer, I am convinced, is yes. There are occasions when the singing becomes very much a "listening for" and a "hearing of" more than the words. There is a mystery here. Music is capable of bearing a mystery. It can create receptivity of the heart to attune to what God may be speaking. Or at least, an attunement that brings a heightened receptivity to understanding particular theological meaning. This leads us to reflect on the fact that when God "speaks" it is more than the utterance of words. In speaking, the musical setting of Psalm 95 recalls the claim that God brings things into being. We understand this when we are attentive and brought to active receptivity of what words about God signify. In this way we can legitimately speak of non-verbal forms of theological perception.

All passionate language and heightened speech becomes musical, or rather, is already musical. There are occasions when the music of earth and heaven meet for us; for example, the Christian celebration of the Easter vigil when the newly baptized come up out of the waters to be received with joy. The image of dying and rising enters into the experience of the whole assembly. Picture the whole assembly beginning to sing "O Healing River" as the ritual movement permeates and the congregation itself becomes a river of grace and joy. The ordered sound, the ritual actions, and the dance all begin to animate one another. In the movement is the hearing of the theology of dying and rising, in the singing is the receiving of the Easter blessing, giving a palpable sense of "becoming alive" reborn into the fullness of belonging to the church as Body of Christ.

I recall another occasion when Fauré's *Requiem* was incorporated into a liturgy for All Saints' Day. In the flow of that liturgy was the naming of all who had died during the previous year. The *Requiem* concluded with Fauré's remarkable setting of "*In Paradisum.*" After the service a woman came to me and said, "I could finally let him go because I knew where he was—in the company of saints. I no longer have to carry the burden of keeping him alive because he is alive in the mystery of God and the communion of saints." There were words, indeed, and prayers, and silences. But it was the music that carried her soul. She found the music opening a form of participation that had eluded her up to this point in her process of grief.

In a recent funeral liturgy the preacher spoke of the movement from sheer sound to music as the place where we find God with us. The deceased in this case was a gifted conductor and keyboardist, one of my former students. The only way to say farewell was to offer the intersection of the music of earth and heaven. But how do we learn to listen for and hear the music as this intersection? The cries of loss and lament, as well as the reclamation of this man's exuberance for life sounded in the music he had given to that church, music that we played and sang. These cries and laments and the joys of naming his life were transposed into the meeting of heaven and earth that permeated prayers, hymns, readings, sung acclamations, and blessings. When the final dismissal came, "Let us go forth in the world, rejoicing in the power of the Spirit," we sang, many with cracked voices, the final "Thanks be to God. Alleluia! Alleluia!" Here was sung theology, and a palpable sense of conjoining our music with the angelic host.

There are music experiences without any texts that carry us to a participation in sheer doxological delight and joy and that tremble on the threshold of our understanding what it might be to join in an eternal song of praise. Theology can sense the limits of language by virtue of the way music conveys a sense of time and pulse and pitch; reflecting but the patterns of how we experience life in time, but also moving us "out of time." Here we may think of Bach's organ works, or movements of a Mahler symphony, or American composer Samuel Barber's "Adagio for Strings" or Aaron Copland's *Fanfare for the Common Man*.

Wordless music cannot, of course, give us what theological reasoning and argument and coherent discourse about God and the world give us. But without music, theological discourse will remain formal, without the affective beholding and receptivity to the larger mysteries of creation, redemption, and a hope for "what eye has not seen, nor ear heard."

There is an unmistakable sense of beholding "what eye has not seen, nor ear yet heard" in and through the music-permeated ritual. The difference between "what you see is what you get" and "what we see and hear is more than the senses can take in" is enormous. This is precisely the difference between living with the "literally given" and receiving the theology of a transformed world. This is hinted at in George Herbert's phrases from his poem "Prayer" when he describes praying as "a kind of tune which all things hear and fear," and "church bells beyond the stars heard."

Theology respects the going beyond words because the object of theology is not captured in the web of language. It is no accident that when poets or great theologians wish to speak of the deepest realities, they move toward poetry and music—heightened speech—as an attempt to "sound" spiritual matters. In moving toward poetry and music to give "utterance" to matters of theology, the greatest theologians also move toward silence in the face of mystery. This silence is not sheer emptiness, but rather a sign of unfathomable meaning, of the intensity of being that cannot be said at all, but only contemplated in awe and wonder.

One of my family's favorite hymns is "In the Bleak Midwinter" set to the English tune, *Cranham*. At the text "Our God, heaven cannot hold him, nor earth sustain..." the music itself bows in reverence before this mystery. Here music can lead us back to a fundamental theological truth, God cannot be contained in human knowing, and will only be recognized when we experience the limitations of our seeing, hearing, and speaking. George Steiner writes, "it is in and through music that we are most immediately in the presence of the ... verbally inexpressible but wholly palpable energy in being that communicates to our senses and to our reflection what little we can grasp of the naked wonder of life. I take music to be the naming of the naming of life. This is . . . a sacramental motion."[6]

What is the "more"? This mystery beyond telling in words? Perhaps we can only acknowledge that human beings may occasionally "hear" the morning stars singing, and the angel hosts, and the voice of God when the songs of earth and heaven converge.

POSTLUDE: MUSIC AS THEOLOGY, THEOLOGY AS MUSIC

If music is intimately related to both body and spirit, there is already a connection with what theology seeks to describe. The human person is such a unity of physicality and spirit, and only in and through the senses do human beings acquire the possibility of a "sense" of transcendence. We are also creatures of time. Our experience of the world and of our lives is indelibly temporal. Music, as we have noted, is the supreme temporal art that may reveal to us, if we are attentive, the very pattern of our living through time. This, too, is on the threshold of religious awareness—the coming-to-consciousness of mortality, but also of the contingency and preciousness of life. Music can give us a sense of our living through joy and sorrow, hope and suffering, passion, delight, and sheer gratitude. Paying attention to how music creates a "sounded" symbolic world may lead to thought. Acoustical symbols are analogous to visual symbols—pointing toward something real beyond themselves while participating in the meaning and the very being of those realities.[1] Here we might say that music offers the possibility of a way of understanding something that language may express but not fully contain.

This way of putting the matter opens the dialogue between theological discourse in language and theological understanding mediated through music. We need not claim that all music is disposed to this mediation. Indeed if what we have explored in these pages is correct, most music does not function theologically at all. The domain of music that sets sacred texts in both liturgical and concert contexts has an explicit connection with the subject matter of the texts. These may or may not be about God or contain specific doctrines. What makes this category of words and music potentially "theological" is, of course, the mode of listening required.

Beyond the matter of musical settings of sacred texts for prayer in hymns, prayers, and liturgical settings, some non-texted music has the power to set the conditions for understanding the mystery of human being, and of being human. This power is found in hearing music without words that has already been associated with words about God. The hearing, for example, of an instrument—say a bagpipe or hammer dulcimer—playing only the melody of "Amazing Grace" at a funeral, carries theological import. Often this can be even more powerful than when the words are sung, and the music itself is the act of prayer. But there are occasions when music not associated with specific sacred or theological texts can be an act of address to divinity. Here we may think of Bach's organ works or movements of a Mahler symphony, or American composer Samuel Barber's "Adagio for Strings."

If music can bear theological import this way, what about theology as language about God, articulated in various kinds of discourse? Can we not say that it cries out for musical interpretation? Is there not something about Christian theology that drives toward poetry and music, and finally toward the deep silence of contemplation?

The fact that theology has generated such an enormous range of music is impressive. But much more than this historical fact, I think, is the claim that theology worth its salt is implicitly musical. When the great Passions of Bach, or the creation by Haydn, or the mysteries of the Trinity set by Olivier Messiaen compel us to enter a deeper knowing of the theological truths, we witness this inevitable drive toward music. But not only in the "high art" tradition of classical music; there is something also of the cosmic energy in John Coltrane's sax, or Art Tatum's prodigious harmonic re-hearing of melodies, or in the singing of Spirituals like "Nobody Knows the Trouble I've Seen" or "Go Tell It on the Mountain" that gives us access to what theology tries to say.

The power of music to awaken us to affective attunement to the created and redeemed order of the world is at the center of what theology has yet to explore in the whole range of music. At the same time, deep attunement to the world is what theology offers in its range of expressions—in language and in art, and perhaps most especially in liturgy. As Mark Wynn has put the point, such deep affections "can provide tradition-grounded ways of reading doctrines in depth, so that they acquire action-guiding force, and take root in a larger self 'of which our intellectualizing is only the thinnest of surfaces.'" [2]

What more can be said at the end of our brief exploration of these themes than this? Music contains more than meets the ear. Theologians, or any who wish to speak of God and the mysteries of human life in this world, can learn much from disciplined, attentive listening to a wide range of music. Not all of such music will be "religious" or set sacred texts. But anyone who wishes to "do theology" as we say, in words, will come to see that "understanding" language about God and human existence before God is often given to us most profoundly when we sing or hear. And, as Dante observed in the *Divine Comedy* centuries ago, and Saint Augustine knew (despite his ambivalence), theology ultimately points toward and participates in the movement and the light, the heavenly music and the dance of being in God. Theology thus ought to lure us to listen for and consequently to hear and see and taste the mystery of our life before the Creator of all things. This requires lament and doxology, the cries of the heart, and the giving way to ecstatic praise.

NOTES

PRELUDE

1. Robert Burton, *Anatomy of Melancholy*, edited by Floyd Dell and Paul Jordan-Smith (New York: Tudor Publishing, 1927), Volume 2, 479.

2. Nicholas Cook, *A Guide to Musical Analysis* (London: Oxford University Press, 1987), 1.

1. SOUND, SYNAESTHESIS, AND SPIRITUALITY

1. Susanne K. Langer, *Philosophy in a New Key* (Cambridge: Harvard University Press, 1942), 193.

2. Gerard Manley Hopkins, *Poems of Gerard Manley Hopkins* (third edition), ed. W. H. Gardner (London: Oxford University Press, 1948), 95.

2. MUSIC AND THE BODY: CHRISTIAN AMBIVALENCE

1. Jeremy S. Begbie, *Theology, Music and Time* (Cambridge, 2000), 271.

2. Ibid, 15.

3. Ibid, 13.

4. Ibid, 15.

5. Joseph Gelineau, "The Path of Music" in *Concilium: Music and the Experience of God*, 202/2 (London: SCM Press, 1989), 136.

6. Begbie, 15.

7. Arnobius, *Adversus nationes* 2:42, quoted in James McKinnon, *Music in Early Christian Literature* (Cambridge University Press, 1987), 49.

8. Albert L. Blackwell, *The Sacred in Music* (Westminster John Knox Press, 1999).

3. THREE THEOLOGICAL AIMS AND MUSIC UNLIMITED

1. Brian Wren, *Praying Twice: The Words and Music of Congregational Song* (Louisville: Westminster John Knox, 2000), 352.

2. Martin Luther, "Preface to Georg Rhau's *Symphoniae iucundae*," 1538, in *Luther's Works*, vol. 53, "Liturgy and Hymns," ed. Ulrich S. Leopold (Philadelphia: Fortress Press, 1965), 321–22, 323.

3. Ibid., 323.

4. Jaroslav Pelikan, *Bach Among the Theologians* (Philadelphia: Fortress Press, 1986), 137–38.

5. Ibid., 138.

6. Ibid., 139.

7. Karl Barth, *Wolfgang Amadeus Mozart*, trans. Clarence K. Pott (Grand Rapids: Eerdmans, 1986), 16.

8. Ibid.

9. Barth, 33, cited in Hans Kung, *Mozart: Traces of Transcendence* (Grand Rapids: Wm. B. Eerdmans, 1992), 69.

10. Igumen Chariton of Valamo, comp. *The Art of Prayer: An Orthodox Anthology*, trans. E. Kadloubovsky and E. M. Palmer (London: Faber and Faber Ltd., 1966), 208.

11. Saint Ephrem the Syrian, "Homiletic Rhythms on the Nativity," selected by Godfrey Diekmann, O.S.B., from the *Oxford Library of the Fathers*, 1847 (St. Paul: North Central Press, 1977), 8–9.

12. Jan Michael Joncas, *From Sacred Song to Ritual Music* (Collegeville: The Liturgical Press, 1997), 114.

13. Paragraph 112 of *The Constitution on the Sacred Liturgy* (The Second Vatican Council of the Roman Catholic Church, 1963).

14. Abraham Heschel, *The Insecurity of Freedom* (New York: Scribner, 1956), 248.

15. This is crucial for any understanding of how chanting and singing theological texts is intrinsic to the meaning of these words. The very "performance" of speaking often hovers on the edge of becoming explicit music. The "music" of a human voice is precisely the key to understanding what is being said.

4. THEOLOGY SUNG: HYMNS, PSALMS, AND SPIRITUAL SONGS

1. Some may recognize that this was Friedrich Schleiermacher's point in considering the "poetic and rhetorical" forms of language (and their embodiment) as the source for more formal theological propositions. Cf. Schleiermacher's *The Christian Faith*, trans. by H. R. MacKintosh and J. S. Stewart (Edinburgh: T. & T. Clark, 1928).

2. Gail Ramshaw, *Words That Sing* (Chicago: Liturgical Training Publications, 1992), 3.

3. Ibid., 157.

4. John Bell lyrics from "Praise with Joy the World's Creator," copyright 1985, The Iona Community (G.I.A. Publications).

5. There is an enormous body of hymn texts that speak of justice. For an excellent survey, see Paul Westermeyer, *Let Justice Sing: Hymnody and Justice* (Collegeville: The Liturgical Press, 1998).

6. WHEN IN OUR MUSIC GOD IS GLORIFIED. Words: Fred Pratt Green. Words © 1972 copyright 1972 Hope Publishing Company, Carol Stream, IL 60188. All rights reserved. Used by permission.

7. The tune *Engelberg* is found in the *United Methodist Hymnal* (Nashville: The United Methodist Publishing House, 1989), while *Fredericktown* may be found in the *Lutheran Book of Worship* (Minneapolis: Augsberg Fortress, 1978).

8. Anne Lamott, *Traveling Mercies: Some Thoughts on Faith* (New York: Pantheon Books, 1999), 47–48.

9. See an earlier title in the Horizons in Theology series by John Caputo, *Philosophy and Theology* (Abingdon, 2005), for an illuminating account of the relationship between theological claims and philosophical reasoning.

10. Wren, *Praying Twice*, 369.

11. GIVE THANKS FOR MUSIC-MAKING ART. Words: Brian Wren. © 1993 Hope Publishing Company, Carol Stream, IL 60188. All rights reserved. Used by permission.

5. SINGING AS POLITICAL ACT: THEOLOGICAL SOUNDINGS OF JUSTICE

1. Paul Westermeyer, *Let Justice Sing*, 40.

2. Walter Brueggemann, *Israel's Praise: Doxology Against Idolatry and Ideology* (Philadelphia: Fortress Press, 1988), 85–86.

3. Nicholas Brady and Nahum Tate, *A New Version of the Psalms of David* (1696).

4. Sarah Ogan Gunning, "Dreadful Memories," copyright 1965 by Folk-Legacy Records, as published in *Voices from the Mountains*, collected and recorded by Guy and Candie Carawan (New York: Alfred A. Knopf, 1975), 114. The lyrics are used by gracious permission of Folk-Legacy Records, www.folk-legacy.com, Box 1148, Sharon, CT 06069.

5. Nimrod Workman, "Don't You Want to Go?" in *Voices from the Mountains*, 156-57.

6. James Cone, *The Spirituals and the Blues* (Maryknoll: Orbis Books, 1972, 1991).

7. Personal interview in 2003.

8. Joshua Dunson, *Freedom in the Air: Song Movements of the Sixties* (New York: International Publishers, 1965), 101; as cited in Don Saliers and Emily Saliers, *A Song to Sing, A Life to Live* (San Francisco: Jossey-Bass, 2005), 141.

9. "Peace Child," in *Sounding Glory: Hymns for the Church Year*, ed. Don E. Saliers (Oregon Catholic Press, 2005).

10. J. A. Olivar and Miguel Manzano; trans. by George Lockwood, "*Cuando El Pobre* (When the Poor Ones)," 1971; trans. 1980.

11. Emily Saliers, "Our Deliverance," 2002.

12. Westermeyer, *Let Justice Sing*, 95.

6. BEYOND "SACRED" AND "SECULAR"

1. For many examples of this critique see James W. McKinnon, *Music in Early Christian Literature* (Cambridge: Cambridge University Press, 1987) and "The Church Fathers and Musical Instruments" in *The Music of Antiquity and the Medieval Period* (Englewood Cliffs: Prentice Hall, 1990).

2. Quoted in Piero Weiss and Richard Taruskin, *Music in the Western World: A History in Documents* (London: Macmillan, 1984), 62. These musical developments soon spread across monasteries and cathedrals across Europe, and eventually became part of accepted "sacred" musical practice. We also note the gender stereotyping here.

3. Jerma A. Jackson, *Singing in My Soul: Black Gospel Music in a Secular Age* (Chapel Hill: University of North Carolina Press, 2004).

4. Ibid., 22.

5. Omar Westendorf, "You Satisfy the Hungry Heart," 1977.

7. LISTENING FOR THE MUSIC OF HEAVEN AND EARTH

1. Gelineau, 136.

2. Ibid.

3. In *Theology, Music and Time*, Jeremy Begbie proposes a careful study of how music uses and creates time and can provide theological thinking with models and other resources for conceiving God's relationship to time in creation. David F. Ford has also offered theological reflection using music as a point of departure in his *Self and Salvation, Being Transformed* (Cambridge: Cambridge University Press, 1999).

4. Jeremy S. Begbie, *Theology, Music and Time*, 273. Begbie cites Bonhoeffer (1972), 302.

5. For a remarkable witness to this hymn, see the video *Amazing Grace* with Bill Moyers, originally produced for Public Television in 1990.

6. George Steiner, *Real Presences* (Chicago: The University of Chicago Press, 1989), 217.

POSTLUDE: MUSIC AS THEOLOGY, THEOLOGY AS MUSIC

1. This definition of *symbol* is derived from Paul Tillich's account of religious symbol found in various places in his writings, especially in his *Dynamics of Faith* (New York: Harper Collins, 1958) and in his *Systematic Theology*, Vol. 1 (Chicago: University of Chicago Press, 1973).

2. Mark R. Wynn, *Emotional Experience and Religious Understanding: Integrating Perception, Conception and Feeling* (Cambridge University Press, 2005), 194. Wynn is quoting from John Cottingham, *Philosophy and the Good Life* (Cambridge: Cambridge University Press, 1998), 165.